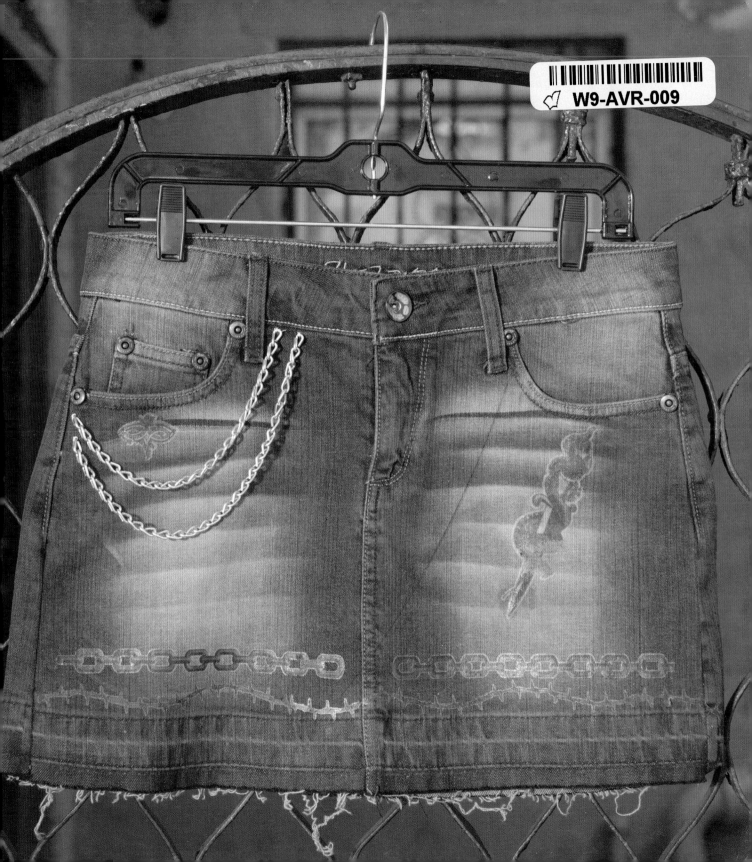

INJEANIOUS

* 52 ways to DIY your denim *

LAUREN A. GREENE

photography by
Sonya Farrell

illustrations by
Kathleen Jacques

WATSON-GUPTILL PUBLICATIONS / NEW YORK

Senior Acquisitions Editor: Julie Mazur
Editor: Cathy Hennessy
Designer: Margo Mooney
Production Manager: Katherine Happ

First published in 2007 by Watson-Guptill Publications,
Nielsen Business Media, a division of The Nielsen Company
770 Broadway, New York, NY 10003
www.watsonguptill.com

Library of Congress Cataloging-in-Publication Data

Greene, Lauren A.
  InJEANious : 52 ways to DIY your denim / by Lauren A. Greene ; photography by Sonya
Farrell ; illustration by Kathleen Jacques.
      p. cm.
  Includes index.
  ISBN-13: 978-0-8230-5108-3 (alk. paper)
  ISBN-10: 0-8230-5108-0 (alk. paper)
  1. Fancy work. 2. Jeans (Clothing) 3. Clothing and dress—Remaking. I. Title.
  TT750.G73 2007
  687'.1—dc22
                    2007001522

Printed in China

First printing, 2007

1 2 3 4 5 6 7 8 9 / 15 14 13 12 11 10 09 08 07

Every effort has been made to ensure that the information presented is accurate. Readers
are strongly advised to read product labels, follow manufacturers' instructions, and heed
warnings. The publisher disclaims any liability for injuries, losses, untoward results, or any
other damage that may result from the use of the information in this book.

dedication

This book is dedicated to the memory of my Poppy Bob, who taught me to see the art and beauty in everyday things and whom I miss very much.

injeanious

contents

introduction

WELCOME TO *INJEANIOUS*. I'M SO GLAD YOU'VE COME ALONG, SO LET'S JUMP RIGHT IN. I've been crafting since I was knee-high, when I sold crocheted potholders and coasters at my family's garage sales. And I've been obsessed with fashion ever since I came home one day from preschool and begged my parents for a pair of Sergio Valente jeans (which back then were a hot new designer brand flying off the shelves). So when I got the opportunity to write a book that combined two of my favorite things—crafting and clothing—I was beyond thrilled! Plus after spending years as an editor at a top teen magazine, I've learned a thing or two about fashion, personal expression, DIY, celebrity style, and what goes into making something hot and trendy. And now I'm psyched because I get to share my experience and insider style secrets with you.

WHY DENIM, YOU ASK? Well, first of all, when it comes to looking hot, nothing equals a great pair of jeans. Like your wardrobe's best friend, jeans are there for you whenever you need them, and they always make you look your best. Even when you've turned your closet upside down and can't find a thing to wear, you can always count on your true-blue pal to give you (and your tush) a major boost of self-esteem!

Denim is also the ideal fabric for crafting. It's like a giant blank canvas just waiting for you to make your own unique mark. Take a look around any retail store and you'll see what I mean. Lately, finding a naked pair of jeans is nearly impossible. Everywhere you go there are miles of jeans, skirts, and jackets dressed up with embellishments, embroidery, bleach patterns, rhinestones, sequins, holes, lace, paint, and everything in between. You could forgo a month's worth of venti iced macchiatos to buy one of these expensive premade pairs everyone else is wearing. Or you could use them for inspiration (like I did) and then build on the ideas to make your own one-of-a-kind creations—you'll save money, have loads of fun, and end up with a denim piece that is totally unique.

After scoping out stores, flipping through magazines, and watching your favorite movie and TV stars for inspiration,

you'll discover that there are a million and one ways to DIY your denim. It can get pretty overwhelming, so I've narrowed it down—to 52 ideas divided into four different moods, or styles. Take the quiz on page 24 to find your category, or just pick and choose projects that catch your eye throughout the book. Before you start one, read the directions carefully to make sure you have everything you need and that you understand the techniques. And don't forget to read pages 12–22 for tips on finding the right pair to start with, on how you go about gathering your materials, and how to do basic techniques like sewing, ripping, and bleaching.

DIY is all about having a good time and letting your individual personality shine through. So keep in mind that this book is just a starting point. Don't be afraid of making mistakes, and don't feel obligated to follow the directions to the letter. Allow your creativity to flow! If you love a style that I used on a skirt but want to adapt it for a jacket, go for it. Or if you see a design on a pair of jeans that would look perfect on your cutoffs, make it work for them. Use rhinestones in place of sequins, ribbon instead of lace, or fringe instead of pom-poms. Listen to your gut and let it guide your work. No matter what you choose, you're bound to look fabulous because the key to looking amazing is: It's all in the jeans!

XOXO,
Lauren

blue note

Wanna do your part to save the environment?
Every beloved pair of jeans eventually fades
away, shrinks, rips in unspeakable places, or
just gets old, tired, and sad—to the point
where no amount of DIY (or TLC) can make it
wearable. But instead of sending used jeans off
to the nearest landfill, why not reinvent them?
Check out the "jeans recycler" project in each
chapter to breathe new life into your baby
blues and keep their stylish memory alive.

chapter

getting

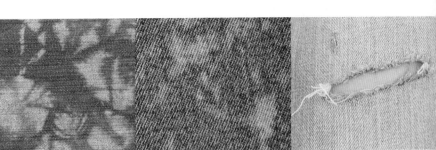

WHETHER YOU'RE WORKING ON A HUGE TERM PAPER OR PLANNING A PARTY you've probably learned that things always turn out better if you put a little preparation into them. And the same goes for being crafty. So before you release your denim diva take a few minutes to read through the next few pages. From smart shopping tips to the right supplies to cool techniques you'll find everything you need to ensure your projects will end up runway-ready.

ready

jeans 101 FINDING THE PERFECT PAIR

The great thing about DIY is that it's a way to reinvent stuff you already have. But what if you don't happen to have any jeans ready to go under the scissors? No problem—there are plenty of places to find free or inexpensive jeans. Or you can hit the mall to buy a new pair. Either way, here are some tricks of the trade designed to help you find a fit that flatters you.

JEANS ON A DIME

For DIY to be fun, you have to let yourself go and not worry whether things will be "perfect". It's better to start your experiments on a pair of jeans you already have or that you got without breaking the bank so you won't be nervous about messing up a new pair. Try one or all of these fun ways to stock up on denim on the cheap.

THROW A RECYCLED-JEANS PARTY. Invite your friends over one weekend and ask each of them to bring a few pairs of jeans or some denim skirts or jackets they are bored with or have outgrown. Put out some snacks, turn on a movie with a jeans-friendly theme (Sisterhood of the Traveling Pants, anyone?), and swap away. You'll discover that one person's trash is another person's treasure!

RUMMAGE THROUGH VINTAGE OR THRIFT STORES. Almost every town has some kind of thrift store, whether it's a huge Salvation Army or a weekend flea market in a church basement. Find one in your neighborhood, and go early and often to get the best deals.

SIGN UP FOR HAND-ME-DOWNS. Ask an older sister, cousin, neighbor, or family friend if you can have any jeans they are getting rid of. Let them know that you are always looking for denim to craft with so they'll think of you any time they have a new batch.

GO OUTLET SHOPPING. Look for an outlet center nearby and make sure it has stores that carry denim. Then grab a friend or two and spend a day scouring the shops for inexpensive but trendy items.

RECYCLE WHAT YOU ALREADY OWN. Go through your closet, basement, and attic and pull out any old denim item you haven't worn in a long time. You may hate it plain, but you'll be surprised how different it will look after you make one of the projects in the book with it. If you find a pair that's already embellished, see if you can remove the stitching or glue to take the decoration off, or cut around it and cover it with a new embellishment.

FLATTER YOUR FIGURE

No matter where you get your jeans, you want to look good in them. These figure-flattering tips will help you look even hotter than you can imagine in your jeans. Find your body type below and opposite, then check out the style secrets for a perfect fit.

PETITE: You want to create the illusion that your legs are longer so that you look taller. Look for low-rise-waist jeans with straight or skinny legs that will elongate your figure. Steer clear of cropped or capri-length jeans and high-rise waistbands that appear to divide you into sections and make you look shorter.

universal fit tips

1. The darker the denim, the more slimming and flattering the jeans will look, no matter what size or shape you are.

2. Treatments like whiskers, streaks, bleach spots, and fading accentuate the areas they cover, so make sure only to buy jeans that have these details on a part of your body you want to put in the spotlight.

HOT POCKETS

No "butts" about it, denim looks sexy on everyone—but a girl can always use an extra little style boost. So consult these tips on picking the most flattering pocket for your posterior!

WANT TO SHRINK YOUR TUSH? TRY:

Pockets that tilt slightly inward.

Pockets that have little or no stitching or embellishment.

Pockets that are a little bit larger and set far apart from each other.

WANT TO LIFT OR SHAPE A FLAT BUTT? TRY:

Pockets with flaps on them.

Pockets placed a little bit lower on your tush.

Pockets that are a bit smaller and have rounded bottoms.

BOYISH: You want to add the illusion of feminine curves. Try a low-rise pair of jeans with a straight leg that will lie smoothly along your narrow frame and won't gap or sag at the waist. Look for jeans with belts, side pockets, pleating, or other intricate details on or near the waistband that will draw attention to your midriff. Avoid looser fits that will swallow you up and make you look shapeless and masculine.

PEAR-SHAPED: Look for boot-cut jeans or a denim trouser with a wide or flare leg. By adding extra width around your lower leg, you'll balance out a fuller hip and thigh area and create a very flattering illusion. Avoid low-rise jeans or jeans with large or cargo-like pockets on the sides that will draw attention to your hips.

CURVY: Flaunt your beautiful curves in higher-rise jeans with straight legs that will lengthen and slim your silhouette. Look for darker denim with a little bit of stretch in it, and avoid bulky front pockets and light-blue washes.

DENIM DOS AND DON'TS

Whether you go shopping for jeans at the mall, the Salvation Army, or your best friend's closet, here are some tips to make sure you come home with a pair you love.

✱ DO: Wear simple, comfortable clothes that allow you to get dressed and undressed quickly as you go from one store fitting room to the next.

✱ DO: Squat or sit in each pair you try on for at least a minute to make sure too much butt or belly isn't sticking out over the top, and to make sure the jeans are comfortable to move around in and aren't cutting into your waist.

✱ DO: Buy jeans that fit and flatter you while you're in the dressing room, and skip that not-quite-right pair you hope will fit later on when you lose two pounds or are less bloated.

✱ DO: Check the zipper. If it's sticking up—not lying straight or flat against your belly—or the fabric is pulling around it, try a pair in the next size up.

✱ DO: Bring a friend along to make shopping more fun and to get an honest critique of your backside view!

✱ DO: Once you've bought a pair, always wash and dry your new jeans before having them shortened. The first wash is when the most shrinkage occurs, so it's best to decide on hem lengths after that's been done.

✱ DON'T: Think you can run into a store, grab the first pair of jeans you see, and be done. Instead, be prepared to slowly make your way through all the racks and try on as many pairs as you need in order to find your dream jeans.

✱ DON'T: Freak out over the size. Every brand is cut differently, so your size might go up or down depending on the label. If a pair of jeans has stretch in it, you may take a size smaller; if it doesn't, you may be a size larger. Ignore the number on the label and focus on the girl in the mirror. If she looks hot, take them!

✱ DON'T: Hem a pair of jeans more than 3 inches. It will change the shape of the jeans and they won't ever look as good. So, no matter how much you love them in the dressing room, pass on them if they are way too long for you.

✱ DON'T: Buy a pair of jeans or a jacket at a vintage or thrift shop if it smells like BO or smoke. If it smells bad in the store, odds are you won't be able to get the smell out even after several washes or trips to the dry cleaners.

✱ DON'T: Feel forced to spend hundreds of dollars to look good. Mainstream stores are starting to design trendy and cool-looking jeans for half the price. Remember, no matter how much they cost, all jeans are made out of the same thing—denim!

the supply closet WHAT YOU'LL NEED

You know how the week before school starts you hit the drugstore and stock up on your favorite new pens, clean notebooks, and pretty folders? There's something exciting about gathering all those supplies and dreaming of the amazing things you're going to do with them. Well, before you start decorating your denim, you may want to head to your local craft store and gather up some goodies for the projects in this book. Also, check around your house since you may already have some of the supplies lying around—and that means you can keep the extra cash to buy cute shoes to wear with all of your new creations!

Here's a handy checklist to take with you when you shop. Start gathering your supplies while you dream of all the fantastic fashions that await you!

☐ **FABRIC GLUE:** Almost every single project calls for glue. It's the easiest and quickest way to transform your clothes without having to sew. Read the labels and make sure you look for permanent fabric glue that is washable; otherwise, your projects will fall apart after a spin through the washer and all your hard work will go to waste. Try Aleene's OK To Wash-It, Beacon Fabri-Tac Permanent Adhesive, or Unique Stitch. These three brands work well and last a long time.

Glue drying times are given throughout the book, but always check the label on the particular glue you are using. The label should also tell you how long to wait before washing your garment.

blue note

Supplies don't have to cost a lot. An old dance costume in your attic may have some great hot-pink fringe you can snip off and use, or a cute hat at the dollar store may have the perfect sparkly pin that you can transfer to a jacket. You might even find a cool retro T-shirt at the garage sale down the street that you can cut up and use. Keep your eyes open and use some imagination, and you'll find craft-worthy materials all over the place!

☐ **HOT GLUE:** A few projects require a hot-glue gun. Use a low-temperature hot-glue gun and low-temp glue sticks to avoid nasty burns. But remember, a low-temp gun still gets hot. Be very careful while you work.

WATCH OUT! Hot glue adheres almost immediately, and it's pretty hard to remove something once it's in place. Make sure you are really happy with the design before you start gluing down the material. Since the glue dries quickly, work on one small section at a time. Hot glue doesn't wash well, so it's best used on projects you won't be wearing (like the Pick-a-Pocket Locker Organizer on p. 48) or don't care about cleaning.

☐ **SCISSORS:** Denim is a bit thicker and sturdier than other fabrics, so make sure you invest in a pair of sharp, all-purpose scissors. They will make it easier to cut a clean, smooth line. And they'll also work well on other types of fabrics and trims. One very important thing—once you get a new pair of scissors to use with fabric, reserve them for fabric only, and don't ever use them to cut paper. This will ruin your scissors and you'll have to get a new pair.

☐ **SAFETY PINS, STRAIGHT PINS, PAPER CLIPS, AND BOBBY PINS:** All these fasteners come in handy if you need to hold two pieces of fabric together while they dry or to keep fabric in place while sewing. Fill a little box or bag with them so they are always within reach, and get something to use as a pincushion to keep your straight pins out of the way and avoid sticking yourself.

☐ **RHINESTONES:** A girl can never have enough sparkle. Rhinestones make the perfect accent for almost any project. You can buy a variety pack that includes a rainbow of colors and sizes, or you can buy smaller packages that are all of one color and size. Keep a handful of rhinestones around to dress up your denim and to take care of repairs if any stones fall off an existing project.

☐ **BUTTONS, LACE, RIBBONS, PINS, ETC:** Keep an eye out for pretty, funky trimmings like these and start a collection—they're great for embellishing any project.

☐ **NEEDLE, THREAD, AND A THIMBLE:** Sometimes you will need to sew by hand, so it's a good idea to have a few basic sewing supplies. You can either use a neutral color thread like beige or white, or find a blue that matches your jeans or a color like yellow or orange to match the stitching around the pockets. Pushing the needle through the denim can be a little tough; a thimble will protect the tip of your finger and make it easier.

☐ **SEAMSTRESS OR TAILOR'S CHALK, OR FABRIC PENCIL:** These can be used to make marks on fabric. The great thing is that they're temporary and wash right out, so you don't have to worry about messing up. Use these tools when you need to sketch out a design or write letters before you go over them with paint or rhinestones. You can also use them when you're cropping a pair of jeans—try on the jeans and make a mark at the length you want them; then use your mark as a guide when you're ready to cut. You'll find these items at any sewing supply or fabric store and some craft stores.

INJEANIOUS IDEAS

While you work on creating gorgeous new clothes, be sure to protect the ones you already have. Wear a smock, an old oversized work shirt your dad might lend you, or a pair of sweats and a tee you don't care about getting dirty.

Work on a flat surface in a comfortable, well-lit area, like at the kitchen table. Before starting any project, cover the work space with newspaper or an old sheet so you don't ruin the furniture or the floors. For extra-messy projects, try to work outdoors or in an unfinished basement or mudroom.

Always wash your jeans, skirt, or jacket before you begin any project so that you start with a fresh, clean canvas.

☐ **MEASURING TAPE:** After spending money on a beautiful piece of fabric or a pretty decorative trim, the last thing you want to do is cut it too short or in the wrong place. Make sure to keep a measuring tape on hand to avoid that disaster.

☐ **FABRIC PAINT:** Look for a variety of colors, textures, and styles, including metallic and glitter paints. If you are going to be outlining or working in a small area, buy paints that come in a squeeze bottle with a tiny tubelike tip; buy larger jars or tubes for bigger projects like splattering or sponge painting. Most paints take about four or five hours to dry, but always check the label and follow the directions for drying and washing.

☐ **PAINTBRUSHES:** Buy a variety pack so you have different-width brushes on hand. Larger brushes work well for splatter painting or brushing paint onto a sponge or stamp, and thin brushes work well for smaller spaces like decorating the edge of a pocket.

☐ **SEAM RIPPER:** When you need to remove back pockets or buttons this little tool can make the job go faster. You can get one at any sewing supply store. Make sure to keep the sharp point covered when you're not using it so you don't accidentally stick yourself.

☐ PAPER PLATES, PLASTIC CUPS, AND PAPER TOWELS: Gather these items when you're working with paint. Use the plates to test out and mix paints or blot paint-filled sponges. Cups filled with water are good for rinsing your brushes, and paper towels are essential for cleaning up drippy messes.

☐ SCRAP PAPER AND PENCILS: You'll want to practice your designs and ideas before working on the denim, so have some scrap material on hand.

☐ TWEEZERS: These are great for picking up and gluing down tiny beads, rhinestones, or sequins. Make sure to set aside a pair just for crafting. Don't use them to do your eyebrows after gluing with them!

☐ BLEACH: Some projects call for bleach. Read the label and look for pure liquid bleach rather than color-safe or diluted bleach. Try regular Clorox bleach, or check with your mom first—she might already have some in the laundry room.

WATCH OUT! Always use bleach in a well-ventilated and well-protected area (outdoors is best), and wear rubber gloves, since it is toxic and can stain. You may want to ask an adult for help with bleaching.

☐ PLASTIC ZIPPER-TOP BAGS: These come in handy for lots of tasks, from organizing and storing small items like sequins or beads to keeping paint bottles from spilling or drying out. Keep a box of them with your craft supplies.

☐ PLASTIC DRAWERS, STORAGE BINS, OR BASKETS: Keep all your supplies neat and organized and together in one area. Lightweight portable storage bins or baskets are great—or even a little rolling craft cart—so you can easily move everything that you need from room to room.

technical school TIPS AND TECHNIQUES

Every good artist knows you start out by learning the basics, then proceed to build on them to create unique masterpieces. Think of the following techniques as the ABCs of denim DIY. Some are used throughout the book, others are extra. Feel free to incorporate any of them into a project to make it your own. Or just use them on a plain pair of jeans that you want to break in.

SEWING

Some of the projects in the book require sewing. If you're comfortable sewing, you can also substitute sewing for gluing in most projects. Sewing will secure the embellishments and trims better and for a longer time.

For this book, you need only two very basic hand-sewing stitches: the running stitch and the basting stitch. Here's how to do them.

THREADING THE NEEDLE

The first step of any sewing stitch is getting your thread on the needle.

1. Get a needle and a piece of thread about 2 feet long.

2. Lick one end of the thread to moisten it, then roll it between your fingertips to make it pointy.

3. Poke the pointed end through the eye of the needle.

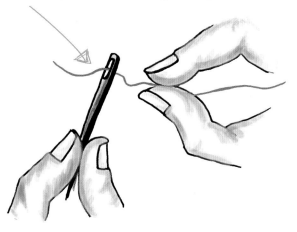

4. Pull so the thread is doubled. Make a knot at the end.

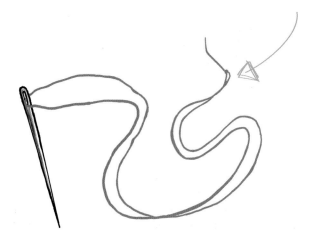

blue note

A few of the more advanced projects ask specifically for a sewing machine. If you are unfamiliar with using one, ask your mom or a super-crafty friend for help. Every machine is a little different, so make sure to read the manual (if available) and follow the directions.

THE RUNNING STITCH

1. Thread the needle and double-knot the ends.

2. Start from beneath the fabric, and poke the needle up through to the top, making sure to catch all layers of fabric as you go. Pull the thread until the knot is pressed firmly up against the back of the fabric.

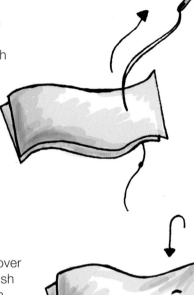

3. Move the needle over about ¼ inch and push it back down through the fabric to create a straight stitch.

4. Poke the needle back up again, right next to the end of the first stitch. Repeat step 3 to create another ¼-inch stitch.

5. Continue weaving the needle in and out of the fabric, making ¼-inch, evenly spaced stitches in a straight line. Keep the thread taut but don't pull it too tight. When you get to the end, tie a double knot to keep the thread from falling out and then cut off the excess.

THE BASTING STITCH

Basting stitches are just large, loose running stitches. Basting is quicker than the running stitch and is used to hold two pieces of fabric together temporarily or help you cinch a piece of fabric to create a ruffle (as in the Disco Vest on page 66). To do a basting stitch, just do a running stitch but make your stitches bigger (about 1 inch across) and looser.

REMOVING BUTTONS

There are two main types of buttons on most denim clothing. You'll need to know how to remove both of them for several projects.

BUTTONS THAT ARE SEWN ON WITH THREAD: Lift up the button so you can maneuver your scissors underneath. Carefully snip between the denim and the button to cut the threads and lift the button away from the fabric. Once the button comes off, pull off or snip away any loose threads left behind. Stitch the new buttons directly over the hole left behind by the original button.

BUTTONS THAT ARE ATTACHED INSIDE THE DENIM WITH A ROUND METAL BASE: These will have to be cut off, since they are fused inside the denim. Snip directly into the fabric as close to the metal base as you can. Cut around the button, again staying as close as possible to the metal edge so you leave behind only a very tiny hole. When you stitch on the new button, you'll have to stitch it to the side of the hole. You can use bigger buttons to make sure they cover the hole, but if you do, you'll need to cut the buttonhole a little with a scissors to accommodate the larger button.

MAKING HOLES

CLEAN HOLES

These are the easiest kinds of holes to make.

1. Take a pair of scissors and make a 1-inch horizontal snip into the part of the jeans where you want the hole. Stick your finger into the hole and wiggle it around to stretch it out a little.

2. Place one index finger along the top and one index finger along the bottom of the hole, and very slowly pull in opposite directions. You'll hear the denim start to tear. Pull a little bit at a time so you don't end up making it bigger than you wanted.

3. When you are done, pull on the white threads around the hole to make it more distressed looking, or if you want a clean hole, snip them off.

4. Throw your jeans in the wash to fray the hole even more.

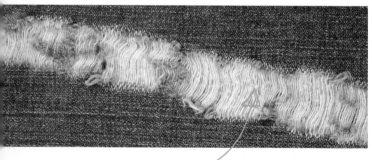

THREADBARE HOLES

Denim is made up of blue vertical threads and white horizontal threads that interlock. To create a threadbare hole, you need to scratch away the blue layer to reveal the white underneath. This process is time-consuming, but if you keep at it, you'll create the impression that you've had your jeans for years and years.

1. Lay the jeans flat on a sturdy surface. Using a serrated knife, carefully begin scraping a small section of the denim vertically up and down. It takes some elbow grease and patience, so take your time and keep rubbing until the denim starts getting very soft and turning white. You may create balls of denim fluff as you scrape. Just peel them off and toss them out as you go.

WATCH OUT! Be very careful using the knife. You may want to ask an adult for help.

2. Once you see the denim whitening, switch directions and start scraping across the same area horizontally. It might be easier if you turn the pants on their side to work horizontally.

3. Keep scraping horizontally, then go back to vertically. Rotate directions every so often until the white threads start separating out. You can speed up the process by poking the tip of the knife carefully in between the threads to help separate them.

SANDPAPERING

CREATING "AGED" PATCHES

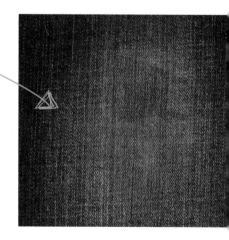

Sandpaper is great for quickly "aging" denim by creating soft, whitish, worn-out patches. Medium-grit sandpaper works best for this, and you can get a package on the cheap at any hardware store.

1. Lay the jeans flat on a hard surface.

2. Rub a piece of sandpaper vigorously back and forth over a small section of denim. Rub vertically first, then go back and sand horizontally over the same area.

3. Continue sandpapering until you are happy with the patch, but be careful not to rub so long that you create a hole—unless you want one! Make as many patches as you wish.

20

FRAYING HEMS AND EDGES

Sandpaper is also great for fraying hems or edges, like around a hole or pocket. This technique helps start the fraying process, but the more you wash and wear your jeans, the more they will continue to fray and the cooler and more distressed they'll get.

1. Tear off a small piece of paper so it's more manageable to work with and easier to get into smaller spaces.

2. Rub the paper vigorously against the hem or edge that you want to fray. Continue until you like the way it looks.

GRATING

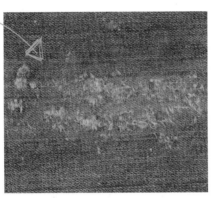

Another clever way to make worn-out patches is with an ordinary cheese grater. It will make marks similar to sandpaper but a little grittier, since the grater has sharp prongs that add more texture. Some graters have several sides with different sized notches. Experiment to see what effects the various sides will make.

1. Place the jeans flat on a hard surface like a table.

2. Rub one side of the grater back and forth over a small area of the denim. Work vertically and then horizontally.

3. Continue until you are happy with the results, being careful not to grate a huge hole through the jeans.

DYEING

You can also use store-bought dye to create distressed looks. Check out www.ritdye.com for great tips on dyeing and tie-dyeing your denim.

BLEACHING

FOR A SPLATTERED LOOK

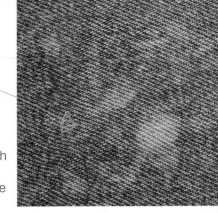

1. Put on rubber gloves. Fill an old spray bottle with two parts liquid bleach and one part water. Shake the bottle to mix.

2. Lay out your jeans (preferably outdoors!) and spray them wherever you want bleach marks.

3. Let the jeans sit for about 20 minutes, then check back. If you still want more whitening, spray another round of bleach.

4. Let the jeans dry flat overnight. When they're dry, turn them inside out, wash them by themselves in the washing machine, and hang them up to dry.

FOR A MORE INTENSE DESIGN

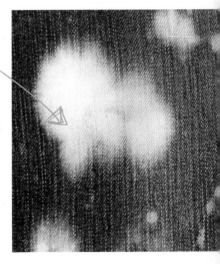

1. Put on rubber gloves. Pour a few capfuls of bleach into a plastic cup. Add 3 teaspoons of water.

2. Lay the jeans out flat. Splash the bleach onto the areas you want to stain. Repeat as many times as you like, varying the splash size to create the desired pattern.

3. Let the jeans sit about 15–20 minutes. Check back and if you still want more splashes repeat the process.

4. When you are done, lay the jeans flat and let dry overnight. Then turn them inside out and wash them by themselves in the washing machine. Hang them up to dry. FYI: you may need to wash them a few times to get rid of the bleach odor.

10 STEPS TO CONVERTING JEANS INTO A SKIRT

Want to make a project that calls for a denim skirt, but don't have one on hand? No problem—just convert a pair of jeans! Check out this 10-step process for turning any pair of jeans into a skirt. And the best part about making it yourself is that you can make it any length that you want.

1. Try on the jeans and mark how long you want the skirt to be.

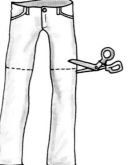

2. Take off the jeans. If you want to leave the skirt bottom raw, cut horizontally across the legs at your mark. If you'd like to hem your skirt for a neater look, cut 2 inches below your mark.

3. Using a small pair of scissors (or a seam ripper), remove all the stitching on the inseams and open up the jeans completely. Be sure to get rid of all the threads. Do the same for the front crotch, but stop at least 1 inch from the fly. Flip over the jeans and use the scissors (or seam ripper) to take out the back crotch seam until the back lies flat.

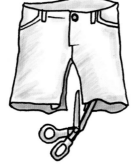

4. Use straight pins to hold the crotch together in front and back.

5. Cut open a large paper shopping bag to make a piece of paper. The longer the skirt, the larger the piece of paper you will need. Insert the paper under the front of the jeans into the V-shaped space. Trace the V-shape onto the paper with a pencil.

6. Remove the paper and, using a ruler, redraw the lines of the triangle 2 inches wider on either side to make the triangle bigger. Cut out the paper triangle—this is your pattern.

7. Pin the pattern to a piece of scrap denim left over from when you cut the legs (or use another pair of jeans); for a different look, use a contrasting piece of fabric. Cut around the pattern to create a triangle. Then repeat and cut out a second triangle for the back. Put the second triangle aside for later.

8. Lay your denim triangle face up, and insert it under the jeans into the V-shaped space in the front. Center it so it's even and there are 2 inches of excess fabric on either side. Pin the fabric in place, making sure to keep the jeans and the triangle pulled taut and flat. It can be a little tricky, so just go slowly and be patient.

9. Sew the fabric in place, about ½ inch in from the edge of the denim. When you finish with the triangle, go back and stitch down the overlapped fabric you pinned near the crotch. Cut off any dangling threads. Turn the skirt inside out and trim off the excess fabric around the triangle, but not too close to the seam you stitched or it will unravel. When you're done, repeat steps 8–9 with the second denim triangle on the back of the jeans.

10. Try on the skirt. You can leave the bottom edge raw, or make a hem. If you want to hem it, have a friend or your mom help you pin the hem so it's nice and even. Carefully take off the skirt. Machine-stitch the hem down. Remove the pins.

the laundry room CARING FOR YOUR JEANS

The best way to preserve your denim is by never washing it, but that's not a very practical option if you want to wear your jeans much. You can extend the time between washes by spraying them with a fabric freshener like Febreze, but eventually they're going to have to take the plunge! These lemon-fresh tips will help give your denim a long happy and healthy life.

CARING FOR REGULAR JEANS

Wash your jeans in cool or warm water, and always turn them inside out to prevent fading.

AVOID USING FABRIC SOFTENER WHEN YOU WASH DENIM. It weakens the fibers in the fabric so your jeans will wear out a lot faster, and you know what that means—a lot of holes in places you might not want them!

TO PERK UP A PAIR OF FADING JEANS OR A DULL JACKET, wash them together with a new pair of jeans. The dye in the new jeans will run off in the water and get absorbed by the older pair. How cool is that?

TRY NOT TO PUT YOUR JEANS IN THE DRYER. Hang them up to drip dry as often as you can. If you need to dry them faster, tumble dry them for 15 minutes or until damp, then hang them up to dry completely.

WANT TO BREAK IN A STIFF PAIR OF JEANS? Turn them inside out and pop them in the dryer with two or three pairs of clean sneakers (FYI: This is the only time the dryer is a good thing!). The sneakers will bounce around against the jeans, beating them up and softening them.

CARING FOR EMBELLISHED AND DIY JEANS

Once you decorate, embellish, and put your heart into a pair of jeans, they may need some special TLC.

Some may still be machine-washable (always turn them inside out first!), but others will need to be hand-washed, or even dry-cleaned. And *all* projects should be dried flat.

Each project in this book has a little icon that tells you how best to clean. Keep an eye out for the icon and follow the washing instructions, so as not to destroy your newly made masterpieces.

dry-clean only

hand-wash, dry flat

machine-wash cool, dry flat

machine-wash cool in a large, mesh lingerie bag, dry flat

find your style

The projects in this book are divided into chapters on different styles, so before you whip out your jeans and glue, take this quiz to figure out which chapter was written just for you. Once you're done, flip to your category and check out a variety of juicy projects. Ready?

1. **You have a lazy Sunday afternoon stretching ahead of you. You can't wait to spend it:**
   a. watching a chick flick marathon and baking cookies
   b. diving into your stack of new celebrity gossip magazines
   c. grabbing a grande mochachino and writing in your journal
   d. sampling new music to download at iTunes

2. **Your favorite thing to wear with your jeans is:**
   a. ballet flats and a fitted cardigan over a frilly tank
   b. strappy sandals and a sparkly tube top
   c. UGG boots and a flouncy peasant top
   d. cowboy boots and a skinny tank top

3. **Your cell phone:**
   a. has a cute photo of you and your BF as the screensaver
   b. is covered in rhinestones and overflowing with text messages
   c. is buried somewhere at the bottom of your tote bag under a sketch book, a bag of trail mix, and a crocheted scarf
   d. has a tattooed skin and a crazy ring, like cats meowing or jungle sounds

4. **If MTV *Cribs* profiled your bedroom, they'd find:**
   a. pastel polka dots mixed with stripes, tiny flowers, and tons of candles
   b. sequined floor pillows and a mirrored dressing table overflowing with makeup
   c. an eclectic mix: Chinese lanterns, a shag rug, and a gold sun-shaped mirror you unearthed at a flea market
   d. black walls, zebra-print bedding, and a shrine to your favorite band

5. **It's your super-sweet-sixteen, and your guy says he has something special planned. You secretly hope it's:**
   a. a moonlit walk on the beach and an engraved heart-shaped locket
   b. a surprise party with a DJ and seventy-five of your closest friends
   c. a picnic in a beautiful park where he'll read you a poem he wrote for you
   d. something unexpected and daring, like paintball, trying a rock-climbing wall, or go-cart racing

6. **It's yearbook awards time. Your friends would elect you:**
   a. Miss Congeniality
   b. Most Likely to Date a Celeb
   c. Most Likely to Backpack through Europe
   d. Most Likely to Go Crowd Surfing

MIX IT UP Are you in between two or even three categories? This quiz is just a jumping-off point, so don't feel obligated to stick to any one style. Check in with your mood ring and make the projects that match how you're feeling that day.

7. If you could raid one celebrity's closet for the day it would have to be:

a. Reese Witherspoon's

b. Paris Hilton's

c. Mary-Kate Olsen's

d. Gwen Stefani's

8. Your dream job is:

a. morning news/talk-show host

b. something fast-paced and high-profile, like fashion editor or celebrity publicist

c. running an art gallery

d. scouting clubs for the hottest new music groups

TALLY UP YOUR SCORE:

MOSTLY As? YOU'RE FLIRTY. Skip over to page 26 for girlish projects complete with ruffles, ribbons, lace, and everything you need to make you cuter than whiskers on kittens!

MOSTLY Bs? YOU'RE GLAM. Check out page 50 for party-perfect sparkles, sequins, and shine. These dramatic, dress-to-impress projects will put you in the spotlight 24/7.

MOSTLY Cs? YOU'RE BOHO. Give your free spirit the ultimate creative fix with all the earthy, artsy projects starting on page 74.

MOSTLY Ds? YOU'RE EDGY. Flip to page 100 for studs, camo, skulls, and other dangerous and daring details that will channel your inner rock star!

level of difficulty

The 52 projects in the book are rated by difficulty so you can know at a glance exactly what you're getting into.

EASY

Anyone from a first-time crafter to a lifetime DIY-er can tackle these simple projects. You'll only need a few supplies and a couple of hours or less to complete them.

MEDIUM

Once you've warmed up on some easy items, you'll be ready to move on to the next level. These projects kick it up a notch and will take you a bit more time.

TOUGH

If you're a crafty pro and looking for a challenge, try these projects. You'll want to set aside a large block of time to do them, since they call for multiple supplies, and sometimes even a sewing machine.

chapter 2

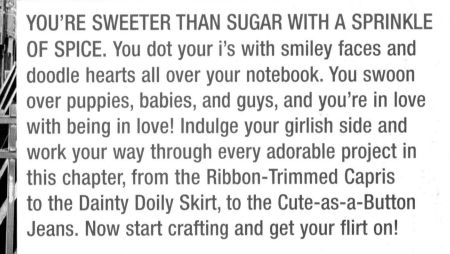

YOU'RE SWEETER THAN SUGAR WITH A SPRINKLE OF SPICE. You dot your i's with smiley faces and doodle hearts all over your notebook. You swoon over puppies, babies, and guys, and you're in love with being in love! Indulge your girlish side and work your way through every adorable project in this chapter, from the Ribbon-Trimmed Capris to the Dainty Doily Skirt, to the Cute-as-a-Button Jeans. Now start crafting and get your flirt on!

flirty

Dainty

Doily Skirt

Better get your grandma on your cell. When you see how cute this doily skirt is, you're going to want to raid her cocktail table for a bunch of these dainty little items. And while you're there, try to snag some vintage jewelry to wear with it! Play up the granny's attic look with a crochet tank top and chandelier earrings, or contrast the skirt's girlishness with a sleek turtleneck and tall boots.

TAKE THIS

* denim knee-length skirt
* assorted-sized crocheted doilies (if your grandma's out of them, check out any local craft store, dollar store, or supermarket)
* washable fabric glue
* scissors

MAKE THIS

1. Lay the skirt face up on a flat surface. Lay out the doilies until you find a pattern you like. Group a few together, or layer a smaller one on top of a larger one. Move them around in different positions until you are happy with how they look.

2. Spread a very thin layer of glue on the backs of the doilies, including the edges. Try to glue around the holes in the crochet so the glue doesn't ooze out too much. Then press each doily down in place.

3. Cut the scalloped outer edge off one doily and use it to trim the edge of one of the front pockets. Glue it down and cut off any excess.

4. Let all the doilies dry flat for at least two hours before wearing.

glue doilies onto skirt

Precious Pearl Jeans

Every girl needs some pearls. Now you can create strands of them all over your jeans with some very cool fabric paint that makes it look like you stitched on real beads. Scatter them across the bottom half of your jeans and accessorize with a delicate lace trim, and you'll look like a precious gem.

TAKE THIS

* pair of jeans
* bottle of Tulip brand Fashion Bead Paint in white (available at most craft stores)
* 1 yard of 1-inch-wide crochet or lace trim
* scissors
* washable fabric glue

MAKE THIS

1. Lay the jeans on a flat surface, face up. Start about 6 or 7 inches below the knee and squeeze out a bead-sized dollop of the paint. Don't press the paint down or flatten it out. Let it dry puffy, the way it is.

2. Continue adding paint "pearls" randomly all over the front of the jeans, from below the knee to the hem. You can vary the size or keep them all about the same.

3. Repeat on the other leg.

4. Add a row of "pearls" along the edges of both front pockets. Be careful not to smudge any of the other "pearls" you've already painted.

5. Let the jeans dry flat for at least 6 hours. Then flip them over and add pearls on the back of the lower legs, following the same process. Let the back side dry flat for at least another 6 hours.

6. Place a thin layer of fabric glue along just the top edge of the crochet trim. Starting directly above the button attach the trim to the waistband, lining it up with the top edge of the jeans. Glue down the trim going all the way around the waistband and over the belt loops, until you get to the other side. Cut the trim and glue the end down in place.

glue trim around waistband

paint "pearls"

Ribbon-Trimmed Capris

You'll be prettier than a present when you wrap your jeans in colorful ribbons. Pick colors and patterns that coordinate, like purple and blue polka dots and stripes, or just pick your favorites. Then wrap away and think of these capris as a gift for your closet!

TAKE THIS

* pair of jeans
* 2½ yards each of five different-patterned ribbons (try varying widths of ribbon from ½ inch to 2 inches wide)
* 1 yard of 2-inch-wide ribbon to use as the sash
* washable fabric glue
* scissors
* measuring tape or ruler

MAKE THIS

1. Cut 10 inches off the bottom of each leg to turn your jeans into capris. (Save the part you cut off—you can use it for other projects later on.)

2. Lay out the five different ribbons next to each other and figure out the order you want them in.

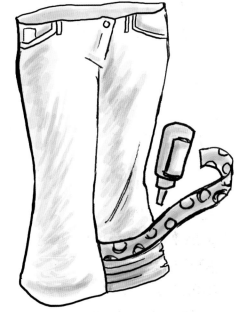

3. Starting from the bottom of one leg, glue the first ribbon completely around. When you get to the end, cut off the excess and glue it down, lining it up with the other end so that it looks nice and neat. Continue gluing each ribbon, one on top of the other, until all five are in place and you've created a wide ribbon trim.

4. Repeat step 3 on the other leg.

5. Slip the 2-inch-wide ribbon through the belt loops and tie in front as a sash. Add a few dabs of glue around the back and sides of the ribbon so it stays in place on the waistband.

blue note

Use leftover ribbon to make a matching headband. Glue the ribbon around a big plastic headband from the drugstore, or just tie a piece around your hair and knot it underneath.

Cute-as-a-

Button Jeans

After a long, hard-working summer, give your white jeans new life in just a few easy steps. And forget about that "No white after Labor Day" rule—you're creating your own fashion, so why not create your own fashion rules, too? Add fun sneakers and a bright tee that matches one of the button colors to turn these jeans into the perfect back-to-school outfit.

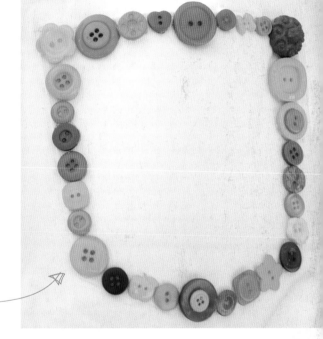

attach buttons around back pockets

TAKE THIS

* pair of white jeans (you can do this on blue jeans, too, but the colored buttons are more eye-popping against the white)
* assorted bright buttons (ask your mom if she has extras lying around, or you can usually buy a big variety pack of colored buttons at sewing or craft stores)
* needle
* thread
* scissors
* washable fabric glue

MAKE THIS

1. Pick out your favorite buttons. Start attaching them randomly around the edges of one of the jeans' back pockets. Some buttons are flat in back, so you can glue those down. This will help make the process go faster. Any buttons that are bulkier will have to be hand-stitched in place. When you are working along the top edge of the pocket, make sure to stitch only through the top layer of denim—don't go through both layers or you'll sew the pocket closed! Continue gluing and sewing until the entire pocket is outlined with a multicolored trim of buttons.

2. Repeat on the opposite back pocket.

3. Using the same process, attach some smaller buttons along the edges of the front pockets to create a cute trim.

4. If the jeans have a button at the waist, carefully remove it by snipping the threads (see page 19). Hand-sew a colorful button in its place.

5. If you use fabric glue on any of the buttons, let them dry overnight to make sure they are held on securely.

Gingham Picnic Jacket

There's nothing cheerier than red-and-white polka dots and gingham. Update an old jacket for spring by cutting off the sleeves and adding these two patterns, and you'll bring sunshine everywhere you go. This sweet little cover-up will look great over a tank top with a khaki skirt and comfy-but-cute sneakers or flip-flops.

TAKE THIS

* denim jacket
* 2½ yards of polka-dot ribbon
* ½ yard of gingham fabric
* red-and-white buttons to replace your jacket buttons
* washable fabric glue
* scissors
* needle and thread

MAKE THIS

1. Cut the sleeves neatly off the jacket, about 11 inches below the shoulder seams. Then roll up the sleeve twice to make a 1½-inch–wide cuff on either side. Place a few drops of fabric glue around the inside of each cuff and press down to keep it in place.

cut off sleeves

2. Remove the buttons on the jacket (see page 19). Hand-stitch the red-and-white buttons on.

3. Take the polka-dot ribbon and glue it down around one cuff. Place the ribbon in the center of the cuff rather than along one of the edges. Glue the ribbon down evenly all the way around the entire cuff. When you get back to the beginning, cut off the excess and glue down the end in place, making it overlap a tiny bit with the other end so that it looks smooth. Repeat on the other cuff.

4. Take more ribbon and glue it down, all around the waistband. Start at one end, placing it in the center of the waistband rather than along the edge of it. When you get to the other side, cut off the extra ribbon and glue the end down neatly.

5. Glue ribbon along the tops of each front pocket, as shown in the photo, lining up the ends with those of the pockets.

6. Lift the flap on a front pocket, then lay a piece of gingham fabric over it. Cut around the fabric to create a piece that fits over the pocket. Glue it down in place. Repeat on the other pocket.

cut fabric to make a piece that covers the pocket

Nautical 'n' Nice Sailor Pants

Want your jeans to stand out in a sea of ordinary ones? Then make these pretty, preppy, nautical-inspired pants. They're perfect for lounging around on your yacht in Nantucket or just hanging out by the pool in your backyard. Pair them with a red-and-white striped tank top and you'll really make waves!

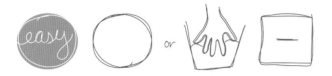

TAKE THIS

* pair of jeans (gaucho jeans look very nautical, but you can use any kind)
* 3 yards of wide grosgrain ribbon
* 1 yard of thick white cording or rope
* 1 gold jump ring (found at any craft or bead store)
* ½ yard of gold chain
* anchor patches
* scissors
* needle and thread
* pliers or pair of tweezers
* washable fabric glue

MAKE THIS

1. Glue the grosgrain ribbon around the bottom hem of each pant leg. Start at the side seam and go all the way around. When you get back to the seam, cut off any extra ribbon and glue the end down neatly, lining it up with the opposite end. Repeat on the other leg.

2. Get more ribbon and glue it around the waistband, going underneath the belt loops. Start directly to the left of the button, go all the way around and stop directly to the right of the buttonhole.

3. Thread the white cording through the belt loops, as if it were a belt. Place a few dabs of glue randomly around the waistband on the ribbon, and attach the belt on top of the ribbon. Let the glue dry overnight.

4. Using a pliers or pair of tweezers, open the jump ring and loop it onto one end of the gold chain. Thread the anchors onto the jump ring. Close the jump ring back up with the pliers so nothing will fall off.

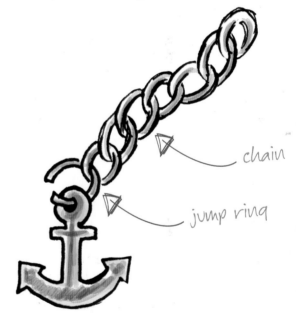

chain

jump ring

5. Hand-stitch the empty end of the chain onto the jeans, directly beneath one of the belt loops. Move down the other end about 4 inches, looping the chain in a U-shape, and hand-stitch it down, leaving the bottom half to dangle with the anchor patches.

6. Put on the jeans and make a loose knot to close the cord belt.

Eyelet Ruffle Skirt

If hindsight is 20/20, you'll definitely be the one in focus when you wear this adorable skirt. By adding just a few layers of sweet ruffles and a couple of tiny pearls, you'll make sure your exit is even cuter than your entrance. Pair it with a hoodie and cozy boots for a playful little outfit.

TAKE THIS

* denim skirt
* 3½ yards of 1½-inch-wide ruffled eyelet trim
* scissors
* washable fabric glue
* 1 yard of thin pearl strand trim

blue note

Pearls can be a little tricky to glue since they are round and may roll around. After you apply them to the skirt, try placing a weight, like a heavy book or a pile of magazines, on top of them to keep them in place until the glue sets.

MAKE THIS

1. Starting directly below the back pockets, measure the width across the back of the skirt. Cut a piece of eyelet trim of that size plus an extra inch. Starting at the left-side seam, glue the trim down across the skirt. Cut off any extra trim and glue down the end, lining it up with the right-side seam.

glue down layers of eyelet trim

2. Measure the width of the back of the skirt again, this time directly below the eyelet trim you just glued on. Cut a piece of eyelet trim this size plus an extra inch. Glue it down across the skirt, lining it up just beneath the first piece of trim. Cut off any excess and glue down the edge.

3. Repeat step 2 until you've covered the whole bottom half of the skirt with ruffled trim.

4. Place a thin layer of glue along the top edge of one of the back pockets. Lay the pearl trim on top and press it down. Cut off the excess and glue down the edge. Repeat on the other back pocket. Let the skirt dry at least 6 hours.

5. Flip over the skirt. Place a thin layer of glue along the edge of one of the front pockets. Lay the pearl trim on top and press it gently down. Cut off any excess and glue down the end. Repeat on the other front pocket. Let dry.

6. Starting under the button-hole, place a thin layer of glue along the bottom seam of the waistband and glue the pearl trim all the way around the skirt, following the seam, bringing it under the belt loops. Cut off any excess and glue down the end.

glue pearl trim along pockets and waistband

7. Let the skirt dry overnight.

some pom-pom trim is
hiding—it really goes all
the way to the bottom!

42

Pom-Pom Jeans

You don't have to be a cheerleader to show off some pom-poms! These flirty little yarn baubles are easy to make and fun to wear. Soft pastel colors like lavender, pink, white, or pale yellow accentuate the pom-poms' girlishness.

TAKE THIS

* pair of jeans
* 3 yards of pom-pom trim
* ball of yarn for the large pom-poms
* scissors
* two pieces of cardboard
* washable fabric glue
* measuring tape

MAKE THIS

1. Measure the length of your jeans leg from just below the waistband to the bottom hem. Cut two pieces of pom-pom trim, each the same length plus an extra ½ inch.

2. Carefully glue the trim down each side of the jeans, right over the side seam. Cut off any excess and glue down the end.

3. Measure the bottom of one leg of your jeans—in the front only. Add ½ inch to this measurement and cut two pieces of trim this length. Take one piece and line it up with the bottom of the side trim and neatly glue it along the front of the bottom hem. Cut off any excess and repeat along the bottom of the other leg.

4. To make the large pom-poms for your belt loop, cut two circles out of the cardboard, each 4 inches across. Then carefully cut a 1½-inch hole in the center of each circle so they look like flat doughnuts.

5. Cut a piece of yarn about 12 feet long. Place the two cardboard rings together, one on top of the other. Thread the yarn through the center of the rings, up and around the top of the rings and back through the center. Keep wrapping the thread until you've covered the cardboard rings completely. This takes a while, so be patient. If you run out of yarn, just tuck the end of the first strand into the wrapped yarn. Then cut a new piece and continue the process, making sure to overlap the new strand over the first one so they blend together.

6. When you are done, snip off the yarn end and tuck it into the wrapped yarn. Carefully start cutting the yarn between the edges of the two rings. When you've cut about halfway around, stop.

7. Take a piece of yarn 15 inches long and slide it in between the two rings where you've snipped. Finish snipping through the rest of the yarn. Then bring the two ends of the long piece of yarn together and double-knot them, pulling them tightly all the way in between the two cardboard rings. This will hold the pom-pom together.

8. Pull the pom-pom away from the cardboard. Fluff up the ends until it's round and poofy. Wrap the long tail of yarn around a belt loop on the jeans and double-knot it so the pom-pom hangs.

9. Repeat steps 5–7 for the second pom-pom.

flirty 43

It's-a-Wrap Sash Jacket

Ever wonder how traditional Japanese brides look so elegant and feminine, all dressed up in their ornate costumes? Capture that innocence and beauty with this unique jacket, complete with an Asian-inspired wraparound sash and decorative accents.

TAKE THIS

* denim jacket
* 1½ yards of printed fabric
* five or six frogs (see p. 46)
* scissors
* measuring tape
* straight pins
* washable fabric glue
* sewing machine

blue note

If you can't find an Anime-print fabric, try another Asian style. Most fabric stores carry a variety of beautiful chinoiserie prints (these are the fabrics that many kimonos are made from), or make a sash out of any fabric, whether it's gingham, polka-dot, floral, or whatever. Check out your local store and see what catches your eye.

MAKE THIS

1. Cut three strips of fabric, each 40 inches long by 6 inches wide. Use a measuring tape or ruler to make sure the pieces are all nice and even.

2. Take one strip and fold down a ½-inch hem on all four sides. Machine-stitch the hems in place. Repeat with the other two pieces of fabric.

3. You're going to sew the three strips together to make one very long sash. First, lay two of the strips together, one on top of the other, with there "right" sides facing down. Make sure the short sides on one end are perfectly aligned and pin them together, about ½ inch in from the end. Machine-stitch your seam and remove the pins.

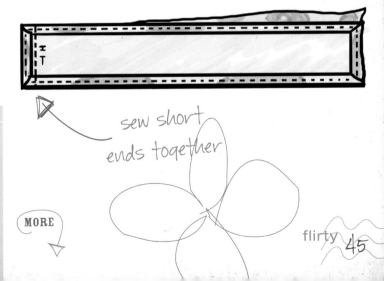

sew short ends together

MORE

flirty 45

SEWING 411 What the heck is a frog?
Frogs are a type of decorative hook that you can use to close jackets, blouses, or vests. They have a loop on one end and a little embroidered ball on the other that you connect together to fasten shut. They are often found on Asian-inspired clothing like kimonos. You can find them at most sewing supply stores. Just ask a salesperson if they have frogs, and don't worry— they won't think you mean a little green amphibian!

4. Take the third strip and lay it on top of one end of your longer piece, again with the "right" sides facing down. Pin one short end of the third piece to one short end of the now-longer piece and stitch together. Remove pins.

sew short ends together

5. Fold your long sash in half and find its center point. Now lay your jacket flat, face down, and find the center of the back. You're going to pin the center of the sash to the center of the back of your jacket. Lay the sash on the jacket, with the right side of the fabric facing up, and align the two center points. Carefully pin it in place.

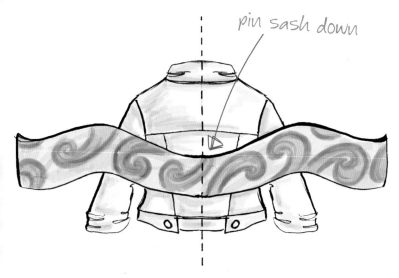

pin sash down

6. Put the jacket on. Wrap the sash around your waist and see if it feels centered—both ends should be exactly the same length on either side of your waist. This part can be a little tricky, so you probably need a friend to give you a hand. If the sash is uneven, have your friend re-pin it in back. Put a few pins along the back side seams and a few along the top and bottom of the sash to make sure it's nice and secure.

7. Take off the jacket. Machine-stitch the sash in place by stitching it up both of the back side seams. Don't stitch across the top or bottom edges of the sash—just along the side seams. You want to leave the back part loose so it gives when you tie it.

8. Pin the sash down on the front part of the jacket on both sides. Machine-stitch across both the top and bottom of the sash to attach it in front. Stop stitching before you reach the button and buttonhole— don't cover those. Leave the rest of the sash dangling.

9. Remove the buttons on the jacket (see page 19). Glue one end of a frog over the buttonhole and the other end of the frog where the button was. Don't glue the loop or the ball down in place or you won't be able to fasten the frog.

10. Glue the rest of the frogs along the front of the jacket. Add one or two over the front pockets or on the wrist as decoration.

11. Put on the jacket and double-wrap the sash around you, making sure it lies flat. Tie the two ends in a loose knot and tuck them into the sash.

JEANS
RECYCLER

Pick-a-Pocket Locker Organizer

You'll be organized 1, 2, 3 with these hot little pockets. Stick them up in your locker, and store pens, makeup, mints, or any little trinkets that usually fall to the bottom. These are made from actual back pockets, but you can also just cut pocket shapes out of any part of the denim.

TAKE THIS

* pair of scrap jeans (one pair for each pocket)
* scissors or seam ripper
* magnetic paper (sold in sheets at most craft or art supply stores)
* hot-glue gun and glue sticks
* rhinestones, ribbons, lace, fabric paint (optional)

MAKE THIS

1. Remove both back pockets from the jeans. Use a seam ripper or the point of the scissors to carefully remove the stitching around the pockets so they fall away from the back of the pants.

blue note

Don't feel like decorating your pocket? Use an old pair of jeans that already has pockets embellished with cool embroidery or fun patches.

2. Place the two pockets together, right sides facing out. Using the hot-glue gun, glue together the bottom edges and both side edges to create a double-sided pocket with an opening at the top.

3. Place the pocket down on the magnet paper. Trace around the pocket with a pen. Cut the shape out of the paper. Peel off the sticky backing and attach the magnetic paper to one side of the pocket (if your magnet paper doesn't have a self-adhesive back you can use a thin layer of hot glue to attach it). If the backing is too big, trim around it so it fits exactly.

4. Decorate the front of the pocket with rhinestones, ribbons, or lace, or label each one with fabric paint or whatever you like.

5. Repeat to make as many pockets as you like, and stick 'em up!

chapter 3

YOU'RE A GLITTERING SOCIAL BUTTERFLY FULL OF CONFIDENCE, CHARISMA, AND ENERGY. Want to make an unforgettable and dramatic entrance? Slip on the rhinestone-studded Sealed-with-a-Kiss Skirt, shimmy into the Fringed Flapper Miniskirt, pop on the sparkly Disco Vest or any other project in this chapter, and when you arrive on the scene you'll drive the paparazzi into a frenzy. Just grab your scissors and get the party started!

glam

Sequin
Garden
Jeans

These jeans are so party perfect, they may try to dance out of your bedroom before you even put them on. With a few yards of sequins and some glue, you can create a sparkly, curly vine that will blossom up and down your leg. Now if only you could grow diamonds that easily!

TAKE THIS

* pair of jeans
* scrap paper and pencil
* seamstress chalk or fabric pencil
* 2½ yards of sequin trim
* package of 5 or 6 mm rhinestones
* washable fabric glue
* scissors

MAKE THIS

1. Practice your vine design on a piece of paper before you start on the jeans. Look online for design inspiration, follow the design you see here, or just make up your own.

2. When you are ready, lay the jeans face up on a flat surface. Use the seamstress chalk or fabric pencil to sketch out your design on the jeans legs. Don't worry if you mess up—all the marks will come out when you wash them, so just correct any mistakes you may have made.

3. Carefully go over the design you drew with glue, then lay the sequin trim onto it. Make sure to glue on only a little bit at a time—the sequins sometimes flip over when you are bending and twisting them into the scroll pattern, so you need to straighten them out before gluing them down. It's not hard, but you just have to be patient. If some of your vines go off in different directions, it's easier to cut separate pieces of sequin trim rather than trying to do it all with one long piece. Just make sure to line up the ends neatly so it looks like one continuous vine.

4. At the end of some of the vines, use the rhinestones to make flowers. Six rhinestones make a nice shape—glue one in the center and then glue five more very close together around it.

5. Line the edge of one front pocket with glue. Press some sequin trim down over the glue. Cut off any excess and glue down the ends. Repeat on the other front pocket. Let your jeans dry overnight.

6. Flip over your jeans. Line the edges of one back pocket with glue. Press the sequin trim down over it, curving to fit the shape of the pocket. Cut off any excess and glue the end down. Repeat on the other back pocket. Let dry completely.

Beaded Jeans

You could spend hundreds of dollars on hand-beaded jeans or spend hundreds of hours hand-sewing beads onto your jeans—but why do either when in just a few easy, inexpensive steps you can create this masterpiece, which will make you look like a million bucks?!

TAKE THIS

* pair of jeans
* 2 jars of Liquid Beadz (available at art and craft stores)
* palette knife or old butter knife you don't use anymore
* washable fabric glue
* 1 package of sequins
* 1 package of rhinestones
* ¾ yard of sparkly fabric
* scissors
* sewing machine (optional)

MAKE THIS

1. Lay the jeans on a flat surface, face up. Scoop a dime-sized amount of Liquid Beadz onto the knife and spread it onto the denim. The beads are gooey and they spread like chunky peanut butter! They don't adhere right away, so you can move them around until you like how they look.

2. Continue adding a small amount onto the knife and spreading on beads until you cover the whole top half of the jeans, from the waistband down to the upper thigh area.

3. Let the jeans lie flat for at least 12 to 15 hours until the adhesive has dried and the beads are firmly attached.

4. When the jeans are completely dry, go back and add a few random rhinestones and sequins in between the beads by gluing them down with fabric glue. Let these dry at least 2 hours.

5. Cut a strip of sparkly fabric 3 x 60 inches for the sash. You can leave the edges raw or fold down a ½-inch hem all around and machine-stitch it down to create smooth edges.

6. Thread the sash through the belt loops. Try on the jeans and knot the sash. If the ends of your sash are too long, cut them to the length you'd like. You can either leave the ends raw, or machine-stitch a ½-inch hem on the bottom of each.

Sealed-with-

a-Kiss Skirt

Cover your skirt in Xs and Os and let it do your flirting for you! Pair this skirt with an equally flirty top, and every time you wear it will feel like Valentine's Day.

TAKE THIS

* denim miniskirt
* lip-shaped iron-on patch (check craft stores for a variety of lip-print styles)
* iron and ironing board (for patch)
* seamstress chalk or fabric pencil
* silver metallic fabric paint
* washable fabric glue
* bag of 6 or 7mm rhinestones
* tweezers

MAKE THIS

1. Follow the directions on the iron-on patch and attach it to one of the back pockets.

2. Use the seamstress chalk to sketch out Xs and Os along the front bottom of the skirt. Alternate between Xs and Os, keeping them all about the same size and distance apart so it looks even. If you mess up, just rub off the chalk and fix the mistake.

3. Go over the Xs that you sketched neatly with metallic paint (leave the Os alone). Let the skirt dry flat for at least 3 hours.

4. Put a dab of glue on the back of a rhinestone and place it at the top of one of the Os. Tweezers may be helpful to put the rhinestones in place. Continue gluing rhinestones until you cover the entire O. Repeat for the rest of the Os. When you finish with the Os, go back and glue rhinestones on the ends of each X, being careful not to smudge the paint.

Victorian

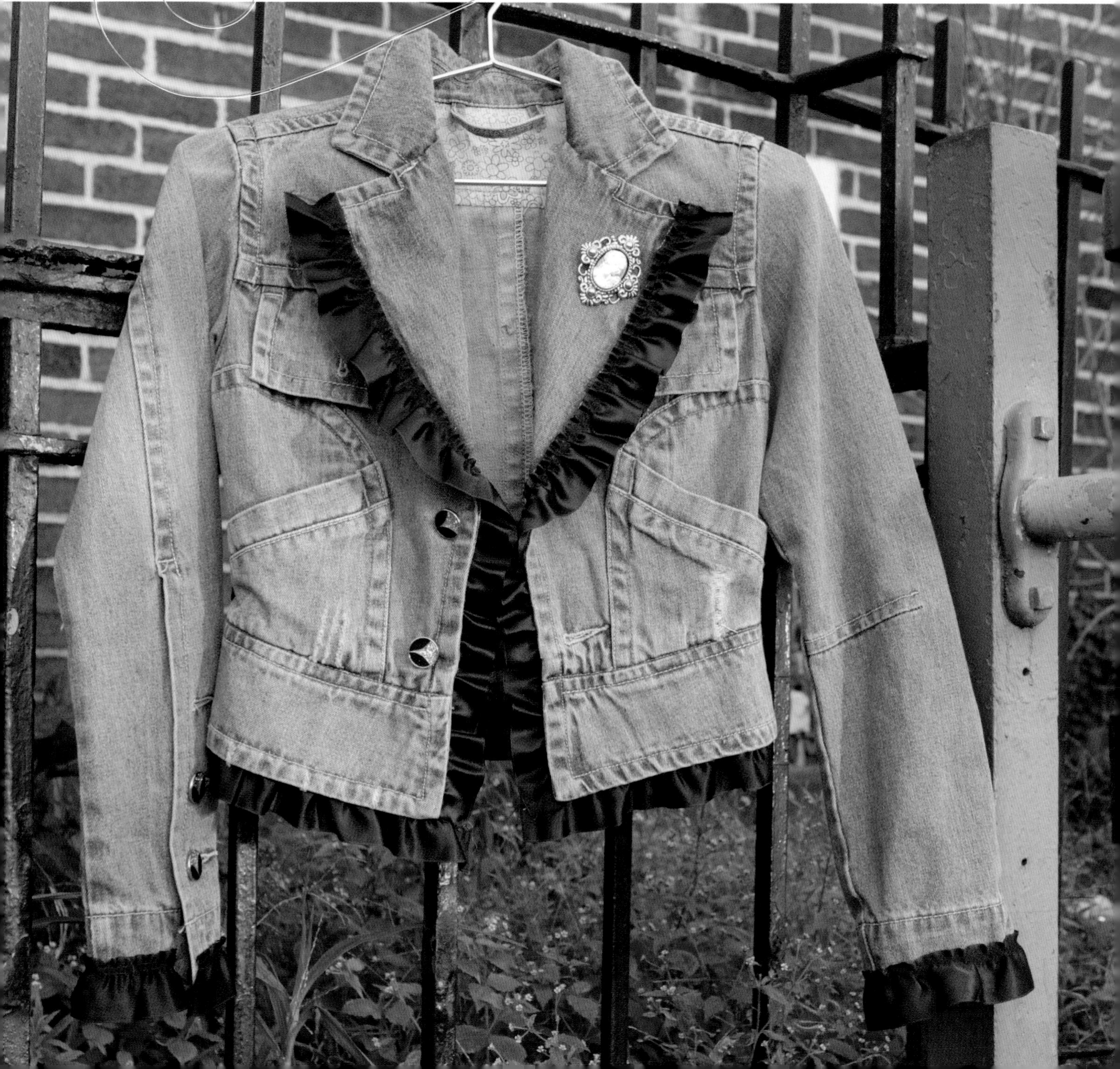

Vixen Jacket

Emily Brontë meets *Sex and the City* in this updated Victorian-style jacket! Thick ruffled trim adds a regal sophistication, and shiny rhinestone buttons make it modern and fun. This piece will look great over a slim skirt and knee-high lace-up boots.

(remove the pin or brooch before dry cleaning)

TAKE THIS

* denim jacket
* 2½ yards of 2-inch-wide ruffled trim
* rhinestone buttons to replace jacket buttons
* rhinestone brooch or appliqué
* scissors
* washable fabric glue
* needle and thread
* measuring tape or ruler

MAKE THIS

1. Lay the jacket flat, face up. Measure the edge of the front, from the very top of the lapel all the way to the bottom of the jacket. Cut two pieces of ruffled trim this length, plus add an extra ½ inch.

2. Carefully glue the ruffled trim down both sides of the front of the jacket along the inside, with the ruffle showing on the outside. Cut off any excess and glue down the ends.

glue ruffle on the inside

3. Measure all the way around the circumference of the bottom of the jacket. Cut a piece of ruffle trim that amount plus ½ inch extra.

4. Glue the ruffle along the bottom of the jacket on the inside. Overlap the ends with the ends of the trim running down the front of the jacket so it looks like a continuous piece of trim. Cut off any excess and glue down the end.

5. Measure around the cuffs, and cut two pieces of ruffle trim that length plus an extra ½ inch. Glue the trim around the bottom of the cuffs on the outside, leaving an opening for the cuff buttons. Cut off any extra and glue down the ends.

glue ruffle around the cuffs on the outside

6. Remove the buttons on the front and sleeves (see page 19). Hand-stitch your rhinestone buttons on to cover the holes.

7. Pin on a decorative brooch or stitch on a rhinestone or glittery appliqué on the lapel of the jacket.

Black-Tie Tuxedo Jeans

Not in the mood to wear a skirt but still want to feel dressed up? No problem! Wear these sleek, menswear-inspired jeans, and you'll turn any event into a formal affair. Pair them with a simple tank top for a casual vibe or go all-out dressy with a sexy vest and sparkly sandals.

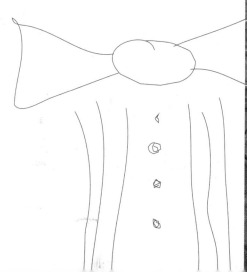

 or ◯ (*depending on the type of fabric ribbon you use*)

TAKE THIS

* pair of trouser-style jeans (you can use regular jeans, too, but they'll look more tuxedo-like and a little cooler if you use trousers)
* 2½ yards of 1⅛-inch-wide black velvet ribbon
* washable fabric glue
* scissors
* needle and thread
* measuring tape or ruler
* 1 large rhinestone button to replace button on fly
* 2 large rhinestone buttons for back pockets (optional)

MAKE THIS

1. Measure the length of one leg, from the seam right below the waistband all the way to the bottom.

2. Cut two pieces of velvet ribbon, each the same length as the seam measurement plus an extra ½ inch.

3. Lay the jeans flat with one of the outside seams facing up. Neatly glue one of the ribbons down. Use the side seam as a guide and lay the ribbon directly over it so it stays straight and even. Cut off any excess and glue down the end. Let dry.

4. Flip over the jeans so the opposite outside seam is facing up and repeat on the other leg. Let dry.

5. If your jeans have belt loops, cut pieces of velvet ribbon the same length as the loops and glue them on to cover the loops completely.

6. Carefully remove the button (see page 19), staying as close to the metal rivet as possible to leave just a tiny hole. Hand-stitch the rhinestone button on to cover the hole.

7. If you want, sew two more rhinestone buttons on the back pockets to add a little extra bling!

blue note

Tuxedo pants don't have to have velvet ribbons. Be creative and try other types of details, like red satin ribbon, gold sequin trim, or ribbon made of interesting embroidery or metallic threads.

8. Let the glue dry for at least 2 hours before wearing.

glam 61

Soho Sponge-

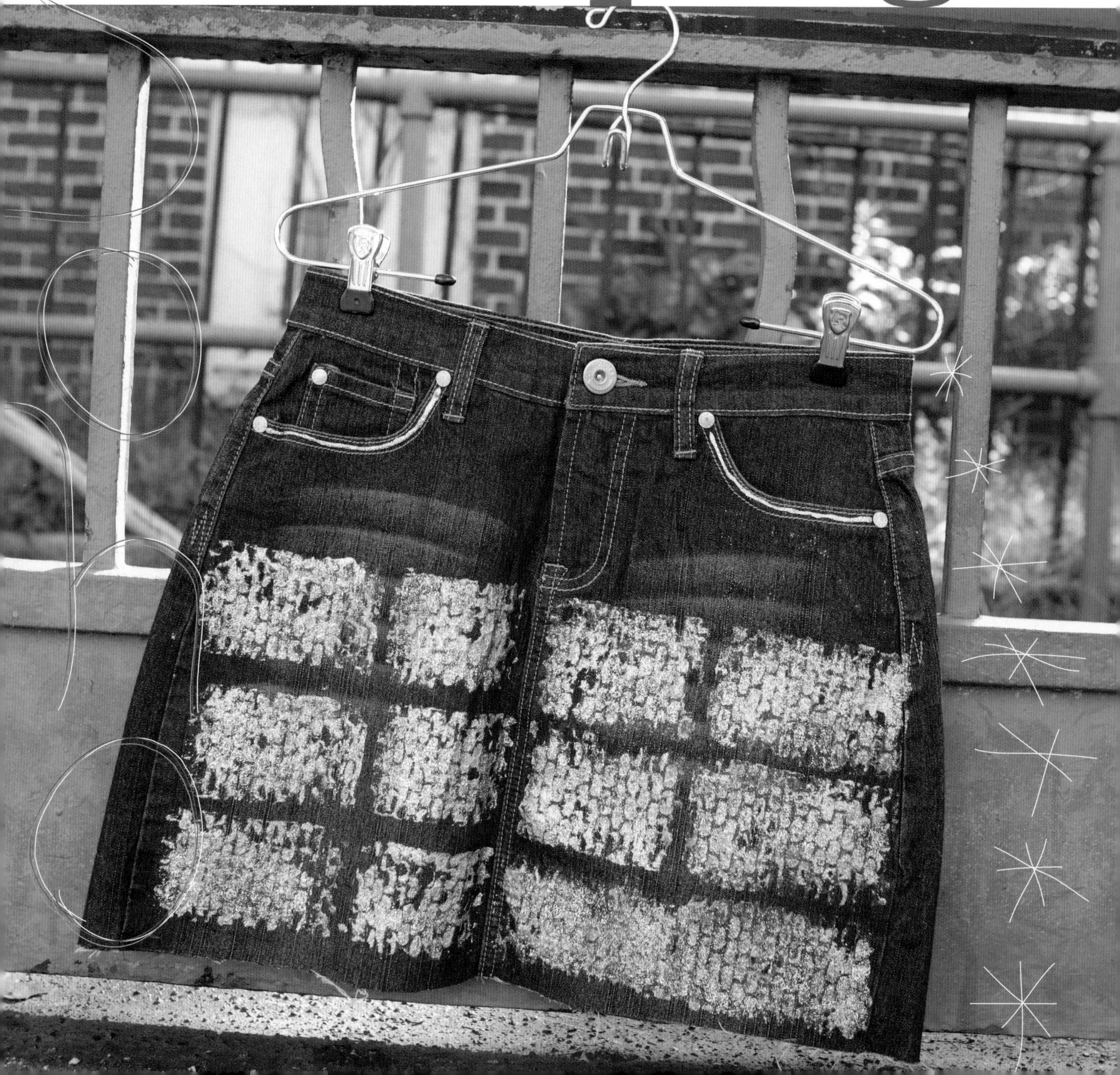

Paint Skirt

Who knew something as boring as a kitchen sponge could help you create unique fashion? The texture on this skirt is so eye-catching that you'll want it to be the focus of your outfit. Keep everything else simple and wear this mini with a black sweater, black leggings, and ballet flats for a very downtown vibe.

TAKE THIS

* denim miniskirt
* assorted-sized kitchen sponges
* silver metallic fabric paint
* silver glitter fabric paint
* paper plates
* paintbrush

MAKE THIS

1. Lay the skirt face up on a flat surface covered with newspapers or an old sheet, so you don't get paint everywhere. Before you paint the skirt, do a bunch of practice runs on scrap fabric so you get a feel for how much paint you need on the sponge and what kind of design you want to make.

2. Squeeze a little bit of metallic paint onto a sponge and then smooth it out with the paintbrush, filling in all the nooks and crannies. Squeeze a little bit of the glitter paint over the metallic paint and smooth that out as well. Repeat if necessary until the sponge is completely covered in a layer of paint but not dripping.

3. Hold the sponge over the skirt in the spot you want to paint, then press it straight down onto the denim. Press around the edges and in the center to make sure the whole sponge is making contact. After a few seconds, gently lift the sponge up, leaving a textured print behind.

press evenly on sponge to create a textured print.

4. Blot the sponge several times on a paper plate to remove any paint, then start again with step 2 to make another print next to the one you just made, or wherever you want.

5. Repeat until you've covered the skirt or created a design that you like.

6. Decorate the edge of each front pocket with a thin line of glitter paint.

add a line of glitter paint.

7. Let the whole skirt dry flat for at least 3 hours.

blue note

The skirt here has a square-shaped pattern, but feel free to experiment. Use sharp scissors to carefully cut the sponges into different sizes or different shapes. Test them on scrap fabric or paper before working on the denim.

Take-a-Bow

Velvet Capris

Gold sequins and rich burgundy velvet make a super-sophisticated combination. These sexy capris will draw attention to your legs, so pair them with your favorite strappy sandals or some great high-heeled boots and take them out dancing or on a date.

TAKE THIS

* pair of jeans
* 3½ yards of 1½- or 2-inch-wide velvet ribbon
* 1½ yards of 2-inch-wide elastic gold sequin trim
* scissors
* washable fabric glue
* measuring tape
* seamstress chalk or fabric pencil

MAKE THIS

1. Try the jeans on and decide how cropped you want them. Make a mark with chalk so you don't forget. Take them off and draw an even horizontal line across both legs where the mark is. Cut along the lines to shorten the jeans. About 10 inches off the bottom is a good amount for average capri-length jeans.

2. Cut two pieces of velvet ribbon, each 20 inches long. Take one piece and glue the end of it just to the left of the buttonhole, leaving the rest dangling. Get the other piece and glue the end just to the right of the button, leaving the rest dangling.

3. Get the sequin trim. Starting on the side with the buttonhole, line up the side and top edges of the sequin trim with the side and top edges of the waistband. (You will cover over the edge of the velvet ribbon—that's okay!) Begin gluing the trim down around the waistband, going over the belt loops, to create a sort of sash. The trim is stretchy, so pull it tight as you glue it down.

4. Go all the way around the jeans until you get to the other side and stop ½ inch to the left of the button. Cut off the excess and glue the edge down, covering the edge of the velvet ribbon on that side.

5. Cut another piece of velvet ribbon, 33 inches long. Measure 9 inches in from the end. Line that point of the ribbon up with the outer side seam and begin gluing the ribbon around the bottom of the jean, leaving the first 9 inches dangling.

6. Glue the ribbon all the way around, stopping 1 inch from where you started and leave the rest of the ribbon dangling. Trim the dangling ends so they're even lengths.

7. Repeat steps 5–6 for the other leg.

8. Put your new capris on, tie all the ribbons closed, and you're bow-tiful!

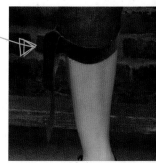

glam

Disco Vest

A denim vest can make you look like a tough chick. Tone down the masculine vibe and glam it up with a shiny mesh overlay and a handmade sparkly brooch. Throw it on over skinny black jeans and slouchy ankle boots, and you'll channel Madonna circa 1985. Material-girl lace gloves are optional!

(remove the pin before dry cleaning)

TAKE THIS

* denim vest or jacket
* 1 yard of lace, mesh, or sheer fabric
* 1 yard of tulle
* ½ yard sequin trim
* leather flower pin (optional)
* straight pins
* safety pins
* washable fabric glue
* scissors
* needle and thread
* measuring tape or ruler
* sewing machine

MAKE THIS

1. You can do this with a vest you already have, or turn a jacket into a vest by neatly cutting off the sleeves at the armhole seams.

2. Button the vest closed and lay it face down on a flat surface. Lay the lace or sheer fabric on the back of the vest to cover the whole thing, or as much as you'd like. Pin the fabric in place with the straight pins. Cut the fabric, following the shape of the vest, to create a piece that will fit exactly. To make it easier, remove a few pins at a time as you cut.

3. Put a thin layer of glue along all four edges of the fabric and glue it down onto the back of the vest. Try not to put any glue in the center if you have sheer fabric or it will seep through and look weird. Let the vest dry for at least 3 hours.

4. Cut a piece of tulle 4 x 15 inches. Run a loose basting stitch along the tulle about ½ inch below the top edge (see page 19). Gently pull one end of the thread to cinch the tulle in and create a ruffle.

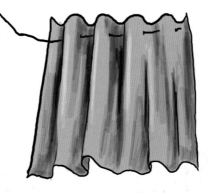

MORE

blue note

Instead of a leather flower, use one made of glamorous faux fur, sparkly sequins, or rich velvet. You can find flowers made from all kinds of fabrics and colors online and in craft stores. Or skip the flower and be creative: use a sequined appliqué, a big rhinestone heart pin, or any other interesting trinket you love that you can glue or pin to the vest.

5. Pin the tulle ruffle along the bottom of the vest on the inside, so the ruffle sticks out the bottom. Machine-stitch it in place. If the ruffle is too short, repeat step 4 to create another ruffle and then stitch it down to cover the whole back edge.

6. Take a small piece of tulle and squish it into a cool leaf shape. (Tulle is very flexible, so just play with it and see what you can make.) When you like the way it looks, safety pin it to the front of the vest. Repeat with a few more pieces if you want.

7. Pin the leather flower over the tulle leaves. Next, fabric glue a few pieces of sequin trim under the flower. Cut up a few pieces of the lace or sheer fabric you used on the back of the vest and glue those randomly under the flower, too, to create a cool brooch.

Fringed Flapper Miniskirt

You'll bring the party everywhere you go with this modern twist on flapper styles of the 1920s. Bright, colorful fringe makes a mini extra eye-catching, and a handful of large sequins adds flash. You'll want to wear this skirt with some dangly earrings and plenty of attitude.

TAKE THIS

* denim miniskirt
* 6 yards of 2-inch-wide fringe trim
* 1 package of paillettes (these are like really big, flat sequins and you can get them at any craft store)
* washable fabric glue
* scissors
* needle
* clear thread
* measuring tape

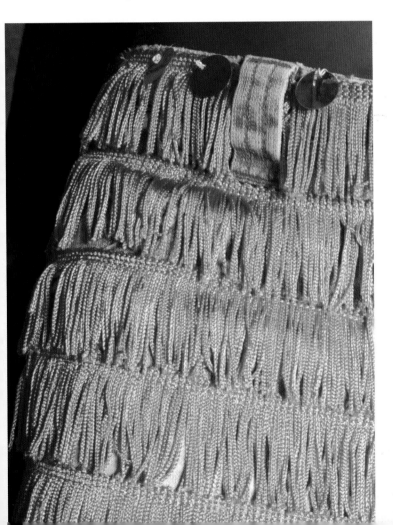

MAKE THIS

1. Lay the skirt face up on a flat surface. Starting at the top of the waistband, measure the width of the front of the skirt. Cut two pieces of fringe each that length plus 1 extra inch.

2. Starting at the left-side seam, line up the top of the fringe with the top of the waistband and glue the fringe in a straight line across. Glue a little bit at a time, making sure to attach only the top band of the fringe and not the fringe itself. When you get to the button you'll need to cut the fringe, glue the end down, and then start gluing a new piece on the other side of the button. When you get all the way over to the right-side seam, cut off any excess and glue the end down. Let dry.

3. Flip the skirt over and repeat step 2 on the back, with the other piece of fringe you cut. Make sure to line up the ends of the fringe pieces so it looks like one continuous piece going all the way around the waistband. Let dry.

4. Now flip the skirt over, move down 2 inches (directly below the first layer of fringe), and measure the width of the skirt again. Cut two pieces of fringe each that length plus 1 extra inch.

5. Repeat steps 2 and 3 and glue down another layer of fringe all the way around the skirt, lining it up directly below the first layer.

6. Continue repeating steps 2 and 3, moving 2 inches down the skirt each time, until you have completely covered the skirt in fringe. Let the glue dry at least 3 hours.

7. Thread the needle and double-knot the end of the thread. Slide a paillette onto the needle and hand-stitch it along the waistband. Repeat as many times as you'd like along the top of the skirt or anywhere else you want a little shine. Slip the skirt on and start shimmying!

JEANS RECYCLER

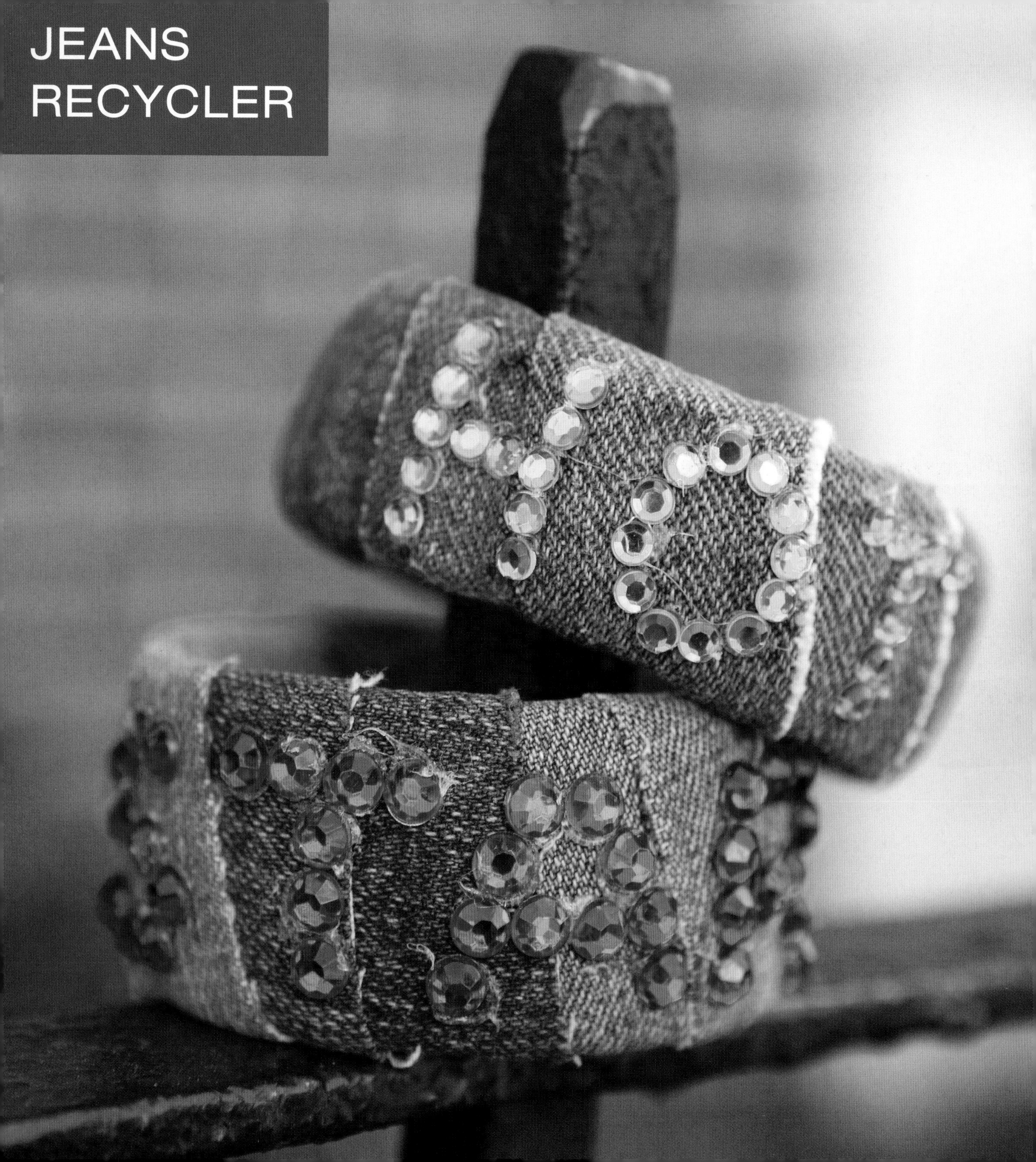

Off-the-Cuff Bangle Bracelets

Bold bangle bracelets are always a chic choice—and when they're covered in denim you can dress them up or down. Add your initials or pick a word ("sexy," "hot," "sweet," "glam") and tell the whole world how you're feeling!

TAKE THIS

* pair of scrap jeans
* scissors
* plastic or wooden bangles (the wider the better)
* hot-glue gun and glue sticks
* package of 5 or 6mm rhinestones
* tweezers
* seamstress chalk or fabric pencil

blue note

This wrapping process is easy to do and works on other items, too. Wrap a dog collar in denim and personalize it for your fluffy friend (just use smaller strips of fabric if you need to), or try wrapping an old leather belt you never wear. A wide denim belt will look great over a crisp white shirt or an oversized sweater.

MAKE THIS

1. Cut your jeans into about seven 1- x 5-inch strips. You may need a few more or a few less strips depending on the width of the bracelet you plan to cover.

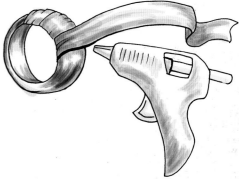

2. Place a dab of hot glue on the end of one strip, on the back side. Attach it anywhere along the inner part of the bangle. Begin wrapping the strip neatly around, overlapping the edges a little bit so you completely cover the bracelet. As you wrap, add a dab of glue under each layer to keep the denim in place.

3. When you get to the end, add a dab of glue and attach the end of the strip to the inner part of the bracelet. Take a new strip and start gluing it directly next to the last strip, making sure to overlap it a little. Continue wrapping and gluing the strips until you cover the entire bracelet.

4. Use the fabric chalk to neatly write out your initials or a fun (but short) word in block letters around the bracelet. Add a dab of glue on the back of a rhinestone and, with the tweezers, attach it at the top of one of the letters. Continue adding rhinestones until you neatly cover all the letters.

5. Repeat with another bangle so you have a set, or make some for your friends as a cute, personalized gift.

chapter 4

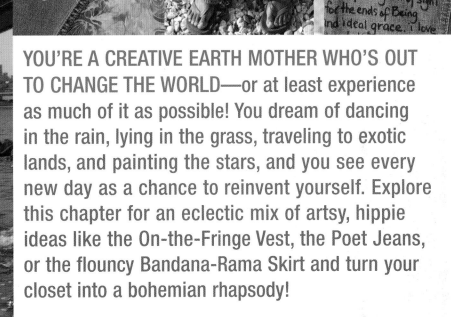

how do i love thee? let me count the ways i love thee to the depth and breadth and height my soul can reach, when feeling out of sight for the ends of Being and ideal grace. i love

YOU'RE A CREATIVE EARTH MOTHER WHO'S OUT TO CHANGE THE WORLD—or at least experience as much of it as possible! You dream of dancing in the rain, lying in the grass, traveling to exotic lands, and painting the stars, and you see every new day as a chance to reinvent yourself. Explore this chapter for an eclectic mix of artsy, hippie ideas like the On-the-Fringe Vest, the Poet Jeans, or the flouncy Bandana-Rama Skirt and turn your closet into a bohemian rhapsody!

boho

Put-on-Your-

Got legs? Then break out your razor and show those babies off in these little short shorts that will become your favorite summer staple. Wear them over your bikini as a cute beach cover-up, pair them with a tank and flip-flops for an outdoor concert, or add cowboy boots and a knotted button-down shirt for a hazzard-ously hot outfit!

Dukes Short Shorts

TAKE THIS

* pair of jeans
* scissors
* sandpaper
* bleach
* spray bottle
* rubber gloves

MAKE THIS

1. Cut the legs off the jeans about 4 inches below the bottom of the zipper to create super short shorts. Flip the shorts inside out. See how the pockets are attached to the side seams of the shorts? Snip them away from the seams until they hang down loose and stick out the bottom of the shorts.

2. Rub the bottom edges of the shorts with sandpaper to fray and distress them.

3. Put on your rubber gloves. Fill an old spray bottle with 2 parts liquid bleach and 1 part water. Shake the bottle to mix the two together. Bleach is messy and smelly, so take the shorts outside or work in an area that is well ventilated and make sure to cover the area with paper towels to protect it from being stained.

4. Spray the bleach mixture randomly all over the shorts. Let it sit for about 20 minutes so the bleach can take effect. Check to see if you want more; if you do, spray them again. Continue doing this until you are happy with the pattern and amount of bleach. Let the shorts dry overnight.

5. Don't wash your shorts for at least 2 days. When you do wash them, make sure to wash them inside out and by themselves. Then put them on and go shake your booty!

To-Dye-For

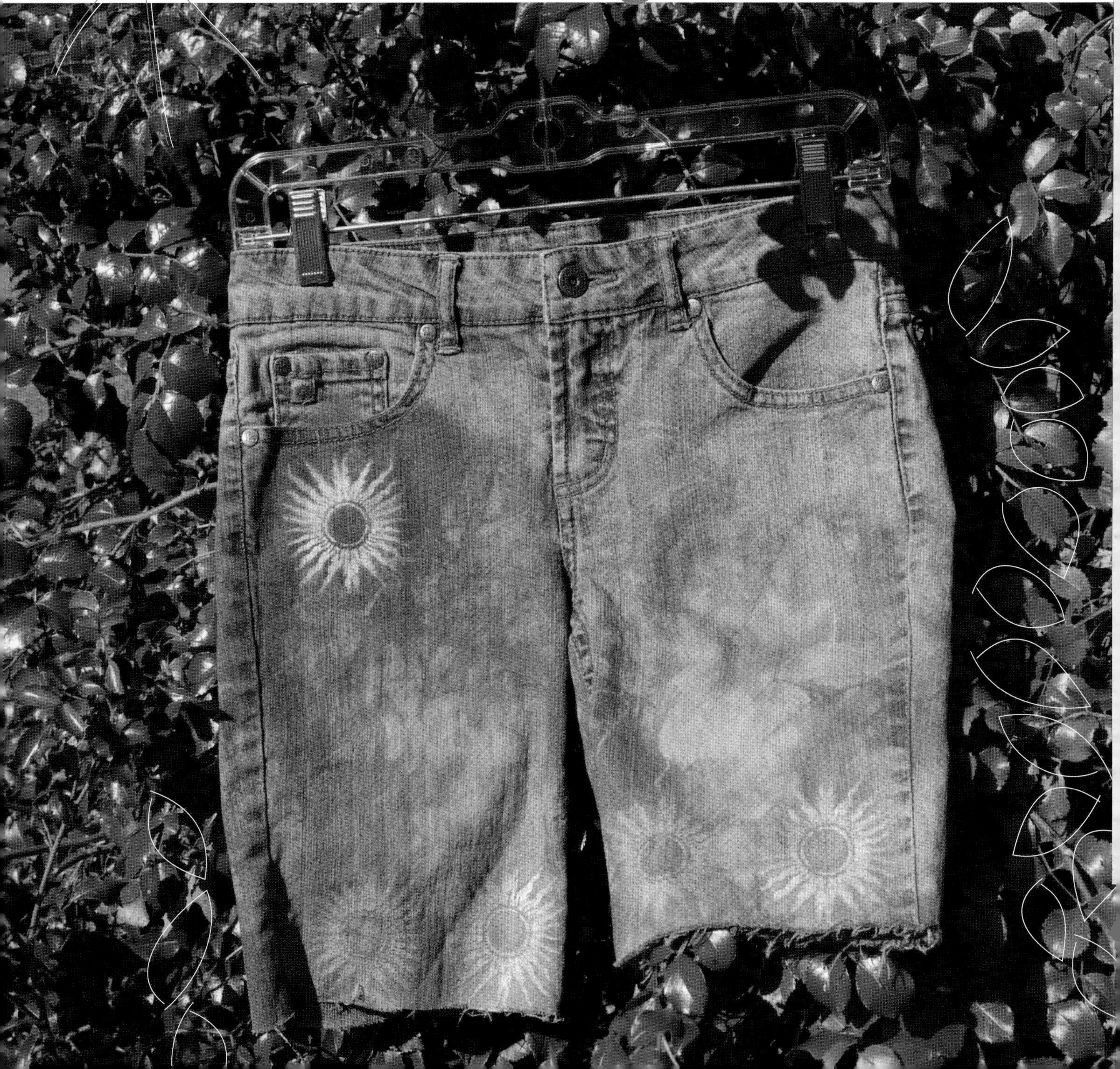

Shorts

When your jeans are looking a little blue, color them happy with this fun arts 'n' crafts project. Turn them into cutoffs, tie-dye them your favorite shade (darker colors on lighter-colored denim work best), and add an exotic stencil. Then pair them with flip-flops, pop a few wildflowers in your hair, and let your spirit run free!

TAKE THIS

* pair of jeans
* 2 packages of Rit dye in different colors
* 2 large buckets
* rubber bands or string
* scissors
* rubber gloves
* long wooden dowel, stick, or old wooden spoon for stirring dye
* old towel
* mild laundry detergent, like Woolite or Ivory Liquid Snow
* stencil
* fabric paint
* paintbrush
* seamstress chalk or fabric pencil
* ruler

blue note

The directions here will give your jeans a cool marbleized effect, but there are oodles of other designs you can make depending on how you fold, scrunch, rubber band, and dip the jeans. Check out www.ritdye.com for other great ideas on how to tie-dye.

MAKE THIS

1. Try the jeans on. Figure out how short you want them and make a mark with the seamstress chalk. Take the jeans off and use a ruler and the chalk to draw even horizontal lines along the mark. Cut neatly across the marks to turn the jeans into shorts.

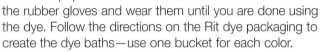

cut straight across

2. This project is messy and stains, so make sure to do it outside or in a basement and cover the whole area with newspaper or old sheets. Put on the rubber gloves and wear them until you are done using the dye. Follow the directions on the Rit dye packaging to create the dye baths—use one bucket for each color.

3. Scrunch up the shorts into a bundle and then randomly stretch rubber bands or tie string all around it. Make sure to crisscross the bands or overlap the string in different areas.

4. Starting with the lighter-color dye, immerse the shorts in the bucket. Let them sit, stirring them every so often for 5 to 15 minutes, until the color is a little bit darker than you want it to be. (It will dry lighter than what you see in the bucket.)

5. Carefully remove the shorts. Cut the rubber bands and rinse the shorts under cool water until the water runs clear. Roll the shorts in an old towel to remove any excess water.

6. Repeat step 3, this time keeping the newly dyed areas tucked inside and leaving more of the blue denim parts on the outside. Repeat steps 4–5 with the darker-color dye.

7. Clean out one of the buckets. Refill it with warm water and mild detergent and wash the shorts. Rinse them again under cool water until the soap runs off. Roll in a towel to soak up any excess water. Hang to dry.

8. Lay the shorts flat. Figure out where you want the stencils. Lay the stencil down on the first spot and paint neatly over it to transfer the design onto the jeans, using the paintbrush to dab fabric paint into all holes. When you're done, carefully lift off the stencil and move it to the next spot. Paint over it again. Repeat as many times as you'd like. Let your shorts dry overnight.

Prints Charming Jeans

Remember how free and exciting it felt to finger paint as a kid? Relive your messy preschool (and preresponsibility!) days with these fun-to-make handprint jeans. Use your own hands or find a friend or sibling to help vary the print sizes.

TAKE THIS

* pair of jeans
* assorted colors of fabric paint
* paper plates
* paintbrush
* newspaper
* scrap paper and pencil
* scissors

blue note
Pastel colors will look great on a darker denim jean; bright primary colors look better on lighter denim.

MAKE THIS

1. Spread out a bunch of newspapers or an old sheet so you won't get paint on the floor or table where you are working. Lay the jeans flat and face up.

2. Trace your hand several times on scrap paper and cut the shapes out. Use the paper hands to plan where you want handprints on the jeans. Move them around to see how many you want and where they should go. When you are ready, leave them in place as markers and then move each one away as you paint it.

3. Squeeze out a silver-dollar-size blob of paint onto a paper plate. Gently press your hand flat down on it and slide it around to cover your whole hand evenly. You can also use the paintbrush to paint onto your hand and smooth the paint out. Make sure to blot away any excess so you don't drip on the jeans. Practice making handprints on scrap fabric or paper so you can see what colors look best side by side and how much paint you need on your hand to make the smoothest print. You can't really fix your mistakes on this one, so make sure you practice until you feel comfortable doing it for real. Use a new paper plate for each new color of paint that you use and wash the paintbrush off, too.

4. When you're ready, repeat step 3 to cover your hand with paint. Keeping your fingers straight, press your hand directly down and flat onto the jeans. Hold it down for about five seconds, then carefully pick it up, leaving behind a colorful print. If there are any holes or smudges, add a little more paint to the area of your hand that needs it and press down again directly over the print. Or use the paintbrush to fill in any holes.

5. Repeat this process to add as many handprints as you'd like. If you want to do handprints on the back of the jeans, let the front dry at least 3 hours before turning them over and painting more. Let the back dry another 3 hours, then try them on and give yourself a big hand for doing such a great job!

Modern
Art
Jeans

Creativity comes easy for a free spirit like you, so splatter, drip, and pour your heart out to turn an ordinary pair of jeans into a walking abstract art exhibit. Throw any rules out the window and go crazy mixing colors, adding rhinestones, glitter, or whatever else you come up with. Wear this *pièce de résistance* with an all-black ensemble (very beatnik!) and give your originality three snaps.

TAKE THIS

* pair of jeans
* assorted colors of fabric paint
* glitter paint pen
* paintbrushes
* plastic cups
* newspaper
* colored rhinestones
* washable fabric glue

MAKE THIS

1. This project is very messy, so wear old clothes you don't care about and try to do it outdoors or in a basement. Put down lots of newspaper and then lay the jeans flat, face up.

2. Squeeze some paint into a plastic cup. Mix in about ¼ teaspoon of water to make the paint a little runny. Dip your paintbrush in, then aim at the jeans and flick your wrist to splatter paint onto the jeans. The harder you flick your wrist the more paint you can splatter. Continue splattering one color all over the pants. Then wash the brush out and start again with a new color in a clean cup.

3. Keep switching colors and splattering on paint until the entire front of the pants is covered in multicolored splatters.

4. When you are done, use the glitter pen to make a bunch of random swirls, dots, and lines on top of the splatters. Glue a few rhinestones around randomly.

5. Hang the jeans somewhere so they can dry for at least 5 hours.

Wild-at-

Heart Jacket

Take a walk on the wild side in this fur- (faux, of course!) trimmed jacket. Animal prints instantly add a touch of the exotic, and when you mix them with denim, black, paisley, camo— pretty much anything—it creates an interesting, eclectic look. A leopard heart on the back looks sweet and sassy, but feel free to be creative and try cutting out a butterfly, leaf, or sun shape instead.

TAKE THIS

* denim jacket
* 1 yard of faux fur fabric
* scissors
* washable fabric glue
* seamstress chalk or fabric pencil
* measuring tape

MAKE THIS

1. Measure the width and the circumference of the cuff. Add 1 inch to the length (for overlap) and use these measurements to cut two strips of fur.

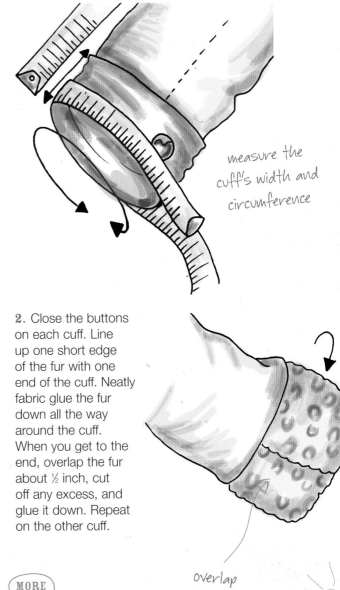

measure the cuff's width and circumference

2. Close the buttons on each cuff. Line up one short edge of the fur with one end of the cuff. Neatly fabric glue the fur down all the way around the cuff. When you get to the end, overlap the fur about ½ inch, cut off any excess, and glue it down. Repeat on the other cuff.

overlap the fur

MORE

boho

3. Lay the jacket flat with the inside facing up. Flatten out the collar. Measure the length and width of the collar and cut a rectangular piece of fur to fit. Line up the edges of the fur with the collar. If the piece doesn't exactly fit, trim around it until it does. Then glue the fur down onto the collar. Use paper clips to hold the collar in place until the glue sets.

glue the fur trim to the collar

4. Lay the jacket face down. Trace a large heart directly in the center of the back with seamstress chalk or trace the template on page 136. Cut the heart shape out of the jacket.

5. Cut a square of fur at least 2 inches bigger than the heart all around. Flip the jacket over so the inside is facing up. Place a line of glue all around the edges of the fur square, on the front. Lay the fur, face down, on top of the hole, making sure it covers the hole completely. Press the edges down firmly. Keep the jacket flat and let it dry for at least 24 hours.

glue the fur to the inside of the jacket, covering the hole

Poet Jeans

When you run out of journals, why not put your thoughts on your jeans? Display your favorite poems, quotes, sketches, and creative outbursts for the whole world to see. The best thing about these jeans is that they can remain a work-in-progress. Add a new doodle during that never-ending history lecture, and let the cute guy from art club write down his MySpace address on your leg!

TAKE THIS

* pair of jeans
* fabric markers in assorted colors
* your favorite song lyrics, poems, or quotes
* friends to help you doodle!
* seamstress chalk or fabric pencil
* ruler

MAKE THIS

1. Lay the jeans flat. Use seamstress chalk and a ruler to create even, "notebook paper-style" lines that you can use as guides when writing out the poems. The chalk will wash out when you clean the jeans.

2. Write your favorite poems, song lyrics, or quotes on the jeans with the fabric markers. This is when you let your creativity run free! Mix up the colors or use the same one. Replace some of the words with little pictures representing the word. For example, if it says "love" or "heart" in your poem, draw a picture of a heart instead.

3. Decorate the rest of the jeans with doodles, random shapes, words, and pictures. Let your friends contribute, or just do your own thing.

On-the-

Fringe Vest

You'll feel like a natural woman in this sexy, earth-mama feather vest. Rock the Native American vibe and pair it with a flippy skirt and fringed moccasin boots. Or throw it on over a sleeveless printed dress and add layers of turquoise jewelry for extra pow!

TAKE THIS

* denim vest or jacket
* 1 spool of thin suede cording
* 1 yard of suede fringed trim
* 1½ yards of feather trim (this also sometimes comes in a package)
* washable fabric glue
* scissors
* ruler or measuring tape
* seamstress chalk or fabric pencil
* silver or wooden beads

MAKE THIS

1. Use a vest or neatly cut the sleeves off the jacket, following the arm-hole seams. Starting at the bottom of the jacket, cut open one side seam about 7 inches up from the bottom (don't go all the way to the top—you don't want to completely separate the two halves of the vest). Repeat on the other side seam.

2. Open the vest completely and lay it flat, face down. Start with one side and line the side seam up so it looks like you haven't cut it. Measure 1 inch down from where you stopped cutting open the seam and make two marks: one ½ inch to the left of the seam and one ½ inch to the right of it.

3. Move down another inch from the marks you made and make two more, directly under the first two. Repeat four more times so that you have six evenly spaced marks on either side of the seam. Very carefully punch a hole through each of the marks using the sharp point of a scissors. Twist the scissors around a little to increase the size of the hole.

WATCH OUT! Keep the scissors away from your body when you make the holes. Denim is a thick material to poke through and you may want to ask an adult for help.

MORE

boho 91

4. Cut a piece of suede cord about 50 inches long. Flip the jacket back over so it is lying face up. Thread the cord through the holes as if you were lacing up a shoe, crisscrossing the lace over in an "x." Loosely knot the two ends together at the bottom. Leave the ends long so they dangle down, or cut them to the length you like.

5. Repeat steps 2–4 on the other side seam.

6. Measure across the back of the jacket, from one shoulder seam to the other. Cut a piece of fringed trim the same length. Glue it down about 4 inches below the neck. If there's a seam across the back you can use that as a guide.

glue two layers of feather trim across back

7. Cut a piece of feather trim the same width as in step 6. Glue it down directly under the fringed trim, letting the fringe overlap the feathers. Repeat with another layer of feathers.

8. Measure across the front pocket and cut a piece of fringed trim the same length. Glue the trim down, lining it up with the top of the pocket. Cut a piece of feather trim the same length. Glue it down directly under the fringed trim, letting the fringe overlap the feathers. Repeat on the other front pocket.

9. Cut a piece of suede cord about 34 inches long. Loop it through one buttonhole and knot it at the top to attach it. Thread several beads onto the ends and make a knot underneath to keep the beads in place. Tear a few feathers off the trim and glue them gently onto the cording.

glue two layers of trim across pocket

Bandana-

Rama Skirt

Bandanas were the must-have accessory for every peace-loving, Woodstock-going bohemian. Add some to your hem and go shake your hippie, hippie hips in this colorful and unique mini. It's up to you whether to glue or sew the bandanas in place, so choose whichever you're more comfortable doing. Give the skirt western flair with cowboy boots and a straw cowboy hat, or dress it down with flip-flops and loose, messy braids.

medium

TAKE THIS

* denim miniskirt
* sandpaper
* 7 or 8 bandanas
* scissors
* straight pins
* washable fabric glue OR needle and thread
* seamstress chalk or fabric pencil
* bobby pins or paper clips
* sewing machine (optional)

MAKE THIS

1. This project works best if the hem on the skirt is raw and frayed. If your skirt has a clean hem, cut ½ inch off all the way around and rub the edge with sandpaper to distress it.

2. Cut the bandanas into about 25 diamond-shaped pieces, each about 4–6 inches wide and at least 8 inches long. Feel free to vary the sizes, and don't worry if they aren't perfect—when they are all placed together you won't be able to tell.

3. You can leave the edges of the bandanas raw or, if you want them to look neater, take each piece, fold down a ½-inch hem on all four sides, and machine-stitch them down or use fabric glue, which will go a little bit faster. If you use glue, make sure to let them dry overnight.

4. Take one diamond-shaped piece and attach the top 2 inches of it to the underside of the skirt, along the front hem. If you use fabric glue, hold the bandana in place with a bobby pin or paper clip until the glue sets. If you prefer to sew down the piece, pin it with a straight pin before you sew. Then remove the pin when you are done.

5. Attach another bandana directly next to the first one, letting it overlap just a tiny bit so there's no hole between them. Repeat this process with each bandana, moving around the hem until you've created a carwashlike effect of bandanas covering the entire bottom of the skirt. If you glued the pieces, let them dry overnight.

6. On the top half of the skirt, draw a 3-inch circle, square, or any shape you'd like with a pencil. When you are happy with the shape, cut it out of the denim. Rub the edges of the hole with sandpaper to create distressed frayed edges.

7. Cut a square out of a leftover piece of bandana that's at least 2 inches bigger than your hole on all sides. Turn the skirt inside out and flatten the area around the hole. Place a thin layer of glue around the edges of the bandana piece and place it directly over the hole, pressing the edges down firmly.

8. If you want another shape on the front or back of the skirt, repeat the process. Let dry overnight.

Rainbow Bright Maxi-Skirt

With a little slight of hand, a sewing machine, and some colorful fabric, you can transform a pair of jeans into an extra-long skirt. You'll love kicking around in this comfy creation all year long. Wear it in the summer with hippie-chic clogs and a tiny tee, or warm it up for winter with a chunky sweater and furry boots. Either way, you'll look magically delicious!

MAKE THIS

1. Follow the directions on page 22 to turn a pair of jeans into a skirt, leaving your jeans full length. But instead of cutting your triangles out of denim, cut them out of your printed fabric.

2. Try on the skirt. It will probably be extra long. Have a friend or your mom help you pin an even hem at a length you like. It's okay to leave it long, but make sure it's not so long that you can't walk safely in it. Take the skirt off carefully. Machine-stitch the hem along the bottom of the skirt where your friend pinned it up. Remove the pins.

3. Add extra decoration if you want. Cut out a few shapes or patterns from the fabric and glue them down randomly on the skirt. Go over them or decorate around them with fabric paint. Let dry overnight.

(tough)

TAKE THIS

* pair of jeans
* 1⅛ yards of printed fabric (batiks are very bright and boho, but you can use any print you like)
* scissors
* straight pins
* sewing machine
* large paper shopping bag or extra-large scrap paper
* pencil
* ruler
* washable fabric glue
* metallic fabric paint (optional)

cut out shapes from fabric and glue on for decoration

embellish with fabric paint

JEANS RECYCLER

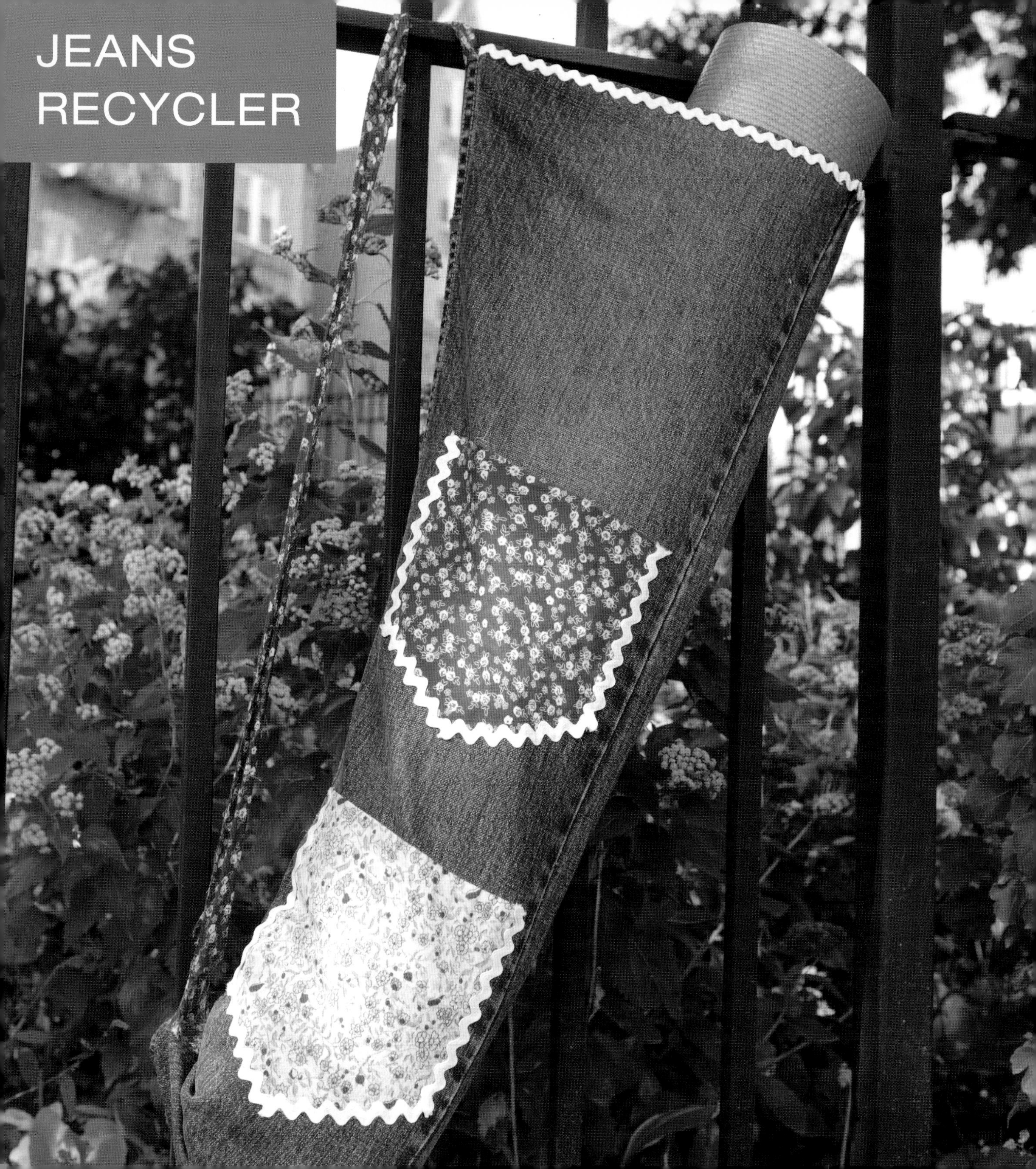

Yogalicious Tote Bag

When your yoga gear is organized in this practical and pretty bag, you'll feel as serene as a lotus blossom! Take it to class and you're sure to get sunshiny salutations from all your fellow yoginis.

TAKE THIS

* pair of scrap jeans
* ½ yard of printed fabric
* ½ yard of contrasting fabric
* scissors
* 1 yard of rickrack trim
* needle and thread or sewing machine
* Velcro tabs

MAKE THIS

1. Starting 1 inch below the zipper, cut horizontally across one leg of the jeans to completely remove it. Trim the length if necessary to create a tube of denim 30 inches long.

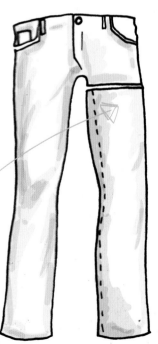

2. Turn the leg inside out. Machine-stitch the bottom of the leg together to close the end. Cut off any excess threads. Flip the tube right-side out.

3. Cut out two pocket shapes, one from each printed fabric. If you need a pattern, cut one of the back pockets off the jeans and use it to trace a pocket shape onto the fabric.

4. Lay the denim tube down flat. Arrange the pockets one on top of the other in the center of the tube. Make sure you leave at least 3 inches between the pockets. When you are happy with how they look, take one pocket and place a thin layer of glue along all the edges except the top. Press it in place firmly to set. Repeat with the other pocket.

5. Glue a border of rickrack trim around the sides of the pockets to decorate them.

6. Cut a piece of fabric 2½ x 28 inches for the strap. Fold down a ½-inch hem on both long sides of the strap and machine-stitch them down in place. Fold down a ½-inch hem on both short sides of the strap and machine-stitch those down, too.

7. Line up one short end of the strap with the bottom edge of one side seam of the bag. Glue down about 2 inches of the strap in place. Pull the strap taut, lining it up with the seam, and glue down 2 inches of the top of the strap towards the top of the bag. It should land about 3 inches below the top.

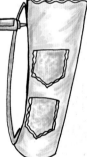

8. Let the glue dry overnight. If you want to strengthen the strap, go back and hand-stitch a seam along the top and bottom where you glued the strap down.

9. Place three or four Velcro strips around the inside of the bag, about 2 inches from the top edge. Pop your yoga mat in the bag, Velcro it shut, drop your gym card and ponytail holder in the pockets, and go!

fabulous

YOU'RE A BOLD DAREDEVIL WITH ROCK-STAR DREAMS. You're always one step ahead of the crowd and never turn down a challenge. For you, life is a soundtrack waiting to be blasted from two-story-high speakers! So crank up the music and check out the fierce projects in this chapter, like the Tattoo You Mini, the Bleach Bum Jeans, and the Cropped-to-a-Tee Jacket, to unleash your inner wild child.

edgy

Serpentine Skirt

Snakes have always been mysterious, dangerous, and intriguing—and you will be, too, when you wear this skirt. Pair it with a fitted tank and some tough-chick motorcycle boots to give the outfit extra fashion venom. Heads will turn when you slink into the room.

TAKE THIS

* denim miniskirt
* scrap paper and pencil
* Scotch tape
* ½ yard snakeskin-print fabric
* washable fabric glue
* scissors
* colored rhinestones

MAKE THIS

1. On scrap paper, sketch out a twisty snake shape about 8 to 10 inches long. Make up your own, or photocopy or trace the template on page 137.

2. Cut out the snake shape and lay it on the snakeskin fabric. Use a few pieces of Scotch tape to hold it in place. Trace around the snake with a pen to transfer it onto the fabric. Remove the paper and neatly cut out the snake.

3. Trace and cut out two more snakes. You can make them the same shape, or create different snake patterns.

4. Lay the skirt flat on your work surface and move the snakes around to see where you like them. Try making half of the snake show on the front of the skirt and the other half on the back to look like it's slithering around you. Or cut one snake in half and show just the head coming out of the back pocket. When you're ready, spread a thin layer of glue on the backs of the snakes and neatly press them down in place.

5. Glue a rhinestone eye on each snake. Let the skirt dry for at least 8 hours, then slither into it and go!

Double-Trouble

Skirted Jeans

Punk up a teeny miniskirt by attaching it to a pair of skinny jeans and loading it up with funky pins. Add your tried-and-true Converse sneaks and your favorite concert tee, and you have an outfit worthy of any mosh pit!

 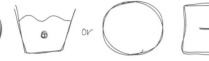 (follow the care instructions on your skirt, and don't forget to remove the pins first)

glue down only the top of the skirt

TAKE THIS

* pair of jeans
* micro-miniskirt
* scissors
* washable fabric glue
* assorted pins
* paper clips

MAKE THIS

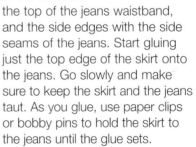

1. Neatly cut the skirt open along one side seam. Line up the top of the skirt with the top of the jeans waistband, and the side edges with the side seams of the jeans. Start gluing just the top edge of the skirt onto the jeans. Go slowly and make sure to keep the skirt and the jeans taut. As you glue, use paper clips or bobby pins to hold the skirt to the jeans until the glue sets.

2. Continue all the way around until the skirt is completely attached. When you get to the button fly, don't glue down the skirt. Skip over it and leave about a 1-inch-long hole or you won't be able to get into your jeans!

3. Keep the clips or pins on for at least 4 hours while the glue sets. Then let the skirt finish drying overnight.

4. Attach an assortment of pins across the front of the skirt.

Superstar Jeans

You already know you have star power, now you can make sure everyone else knows it, too. Make these über-cool jeans that will have everyone wondering if you're with the band. Then wear them while perfecting your air guitar and get ready to fend off the groupies.

TAKE THIS

* pair of jeans
* old pair of jeans or scrap denim
* scissors
* scrap paper
* pencil
* sandpaper
* washable fabric glue

MAKE THIS

1. Sketch two star shapes on scrap paper, one large and one smaller. You can draw your own, or use the templates on page 138. Cut them out of the paper.

2. Pin a paper star onto your scrap jeans. Trace around it to transfer the shape onto the denim. Cut the star out of the denim. Repeat until you have four larger stars and four smaller stars.

3. Rub the sandpaper briskly along the edges of each star to fray the denim and make it look fringy and distressed.

4. Layer one smaller star on top of one larger star and glue it down. To get two-toned stars like you see in the photos, use one star right-side up and one star right-side down. Repeat with the other stars.

5. Remove the back pockets from your jeans. Use a seam ripper to carefully remove the stitches that hold the pocket to the jeans. Once you do, the pockets should fall off easily. If there are any rivets in the top corners of the pockets, you'll have to leave those behind, but they will add to the effect, so don't worry!

6. Glue a layered star in the space where each back pocket was.

7. Glue the remaining layered stars onto the front of the right leg, as in the photos.

8. Make a rip in the left knee. See page 20 for directions on how to make a clean or threadbare hole.

edgy 107

Bleach

Bum Jeans

Make a splashy statement in these bold jeans—they'll make you want to party like a rock star! They're easy to create but look like they were custom-made especially for you. Promise to make your friends a pair, and you may have a few willing roadies to help any time you take your jeans on tour!

TAKE THIS

* pair of dark denim jeans
* bottle of bleach
* rubber gloves
* plastic cup
* seamstress chalk or fabric pencil
* washable fabric glue
* tweezers
* 1 package of small rhinestones

MAKE THIS

1. Bleach is messy, it stains, and it's toxic, so make sure to do this project outside or in a very well-ventilated area that you don't mind getting dirty or staining. If you have to do it inside, cover your work space with a thick layer of old sheets, heavy-duty garbage bags, or an old shower curtain to catch the excess bleach that will leak off the sides of the jeans.

2. Lay the jeans on your work surface face up and flat. Put on the rubber gloves and open the bleach.

3. Pour a few capfuls of bleach into a plastic cup. Carefully splash the bleach onto the jeans and let it sit. Repeat all over the jeans, making some bigger splashes with more bleach and some smaller splashes with less bleach to create a random pattern. It's hard to control the pattern, so just let it splash wherever it goes and try not to worry about it looking a certain way. Stop frequently and let the jeans sit for about 15 minutes for the full bleach effect to appear before doing more, so you can see what it looks like and don't end up putting on too much.

4. Continue adding and then letting it sit until you like the way it looks. Flip over the jeans and repeat on the back.

5. Hang the jeans to dry overnight either outside or in the laundry room. Be warned, they are going to smell pretty strong (like a pool), so don't bring them all over the house!

6. The next day, turn them inside out and wash them by themselves in the washing machine. Then hang them up to dry.

7. When they are dry, lay them flat, face down. Pick a word you like and draw the letters across the tush with seamstress chalk. (Don't worry if you mess up—the chalk comes out in the wash, so just go over any of your mistakes.)

8. When you are all set and the letters look even, go over one letter with a thin layer of glue. Use the tweezers to pick up a rhinestone and place it on  the glue. Continue until you've covered the entire letter. Repeat until the whole word is spelled out in rhinestones.

9. Let dry for at least 5 hours before wearing. The jeans may still smell a bit, so they might need another wash, or you can throw them in the dryer on "fluff" with a dryer sheet to sweeten them up. And make sure that for the next three or four times you wash them, you keep them separate. Some of the bleach may continue to run off a bit, so you want to avoid bleaching any other clothing.

Tee Jacket

Play "pin the tee on the jacket"! Cut up an old band T-shirt and rearrange the letters or images on the back of a denim jacket. Then crop it, layer it over a graphic top, and add a pile of silver chains. You'll be ready to rock out at your favorite concert or just hang out at the mall.

TAKE THIS

* denim jacket
* old T-shirt with graphics or letters
* black or gray fabric paint
* plastic cup
* sandpaper
* ruler
* seamstress chalk or fabric pencil
* scissors
* paintbrush
* paper towels
* fabric glue
* white or silver fabric paint (optional)

MAKE THIS

1. Try on your jacket. Figure out how cropped you want the bottom to be and make a mark with the chalk. Take off the jacket and use the ruler to draw an even horizontal line across the jacket at the level of the mark.

2. Cut across the line to shorten the jacket. Rub the hemline briskly with sandpaper to fray the edges. Pull on the threads that are hanging out to make them longer and to unravel the hem. Run the jacket through the wash to beat up the hem even more. Let it air-dry.

cut jacket straight across

3. Place the jacket flat on top of newspapers or old sheets so you don't get paint all over your work space. Squeeze out some black or gray fabric paint into a plastic cup. Dip the paintbrush in and then splatter it or brush it in quick strokes onto the jacket. Repeat several times until you've randomly covered the front of the jacket in bold paint marks. Then take a moist paper towel and go over all the marks, gently rubbing them in to create the effect of an oil spill or grease-mark. Let dry 2 hours.

4. Cut out the letters or a picture from a cool rock T-shirt. Use an old tee you don't wear anymore, or check out a thrift shop or vintage store to find some that you like. Figure out exactly where you want to place the letters or the picture on the back of the jacket. Then line the edges of each letter with a thin layer of glue and press it in place. Let dry 3 hours.

5. If you want, outline each letter with a thin line of white or silver fabric paint so they really pop off the jacket.

rub on gray paint for an oil-spill effect

Tattoo You Skirt

Tattooing yourself may not go over well with the folks, but tattooing your jeans will. Use temporary tats to create an artful masterpiece that will rival the forearms of any punk band drummer! Wear the skirt with leggings, chunky boots, and a tank, and make sure to save one of those tats for your own arm.

TAKE THIS

* denim skirt
* several different temporary tattoos
* scissors
* old towel
* washcloth
* clear nail polish
* 1 yard of thin chain link (you can get this at any hardware store; when you buy it, ask the salesperson to cut it into an 8-inch-long piece and a 10-inch-long piece).
* needle and thread
* pliers (if needed to cut the chain)

MAKE THIS

1. Place the tattoos on the skirt and move them around until you like how they look. This works best on a very flat surface, so try not to use them on the waistband or on any textured part of the denim, like over the zipper, or over a seam.

2. When you decide on a design, take the first tattoo and cut around it, leaving a ¼-inch border. Place a large towel down on the counter and lay the skirt on top. Remove the clear plastic top sheet from the first tattoo and place it face down on the skirt, wherever you want it, then soak the back of it with a very wet washcloth. Make sure the tattoo is good and wet, then press the washcloth down on top of it to hold it in place and keep it moist.

3. Hold the cloth down for about a minute. Then very gently remove it. Carefully lift up one end of the tattoo and see if it has attached to the jeans. If not, press it back down and let it sit for another 30 seconds. Then lift the paper up very slowly and evenly, leaving behind the tattoo on the jeans.

4. Repeat for as many tattoos as you want. Lay the skirt flat and let it dry at least 24 hours.

5. When it's completely dry, apply a very thin layer of clear nail polish directly over each tattoo. Let dry flat at least another 24 hours. Apply one more coat of polish and let dry another 24 hours.

6. If your chain wasn't cut by the salesperson, use a pliers to open one of the links and separate it from the chain in order to "cut" it. Cut two pieces: one 8 inches long and one 10 inches long.

7. Hand-stitch one end of the 8-inch chain directly under the waistband, 2 or 3 inches to the left of the zipper. Drape it under the pocket and hand-stitch the other side of the chain right under the pocket near the side seam. Repeat with the longer chain so it drapes directly under the first chain.

Punky Pirate Jeans

Johnny Depp proved that nothing's hotter than a pirate. You'll be sizzling, too, in these wicked jeans. With a little bleach and a stencil, you can create the very cool universal symbol for danger. Slink into these pants, add a striped tee and some heavy-metal accessories, and people had better watch out when they see you coming. *Argh!*

TAKE THIS

* pair of dark blue or black jeans
* skull-and-crossbones stencil (buy one, make your own with scrap paper and a thin piece of cardboard, or use template on page 139)
* scissors
* pencil
* Scotch tape
* Clorox bleach pen (found in the detergent aisle of most supermarkets)
* rubber gloves
* white fabric paint and paintbrush
* skull-and-crossbones suspenders (optional)

MAKE THIS

1. If you bought a stencil, skip to step 4. If you don't have one, just make it yourself! Start by tracing the template from page 139 onto scrap paper.

2. Cut the shape out neatly. You want to cut out the inside of the shape, leaving a skull-shaped hole. Start by poking your scissors into the skull shape to make a hole, then carefully cut out the shape. Then cut out the eyes and nose shapes. Tape the skull-shaped hole to a piece of thin cardboard.  Put some tape around your finger and make tape rings. Stick them on the back of the pieces for the eyes and nose and place them in the center where they should go. Trace around the cutout and pieces to transfer everything onto the cardboard. Remove the paper.

3. Now cut the skull shape out of the cardboard. Again, cut out the inside of the shape. Start by poking your scissors into the center. Be careful when cutting out the eyes and nose, and save the pieces you cut out.

4. Take your jeans outside or to a well-ventilated work space and lay them flat, face up. Decide where you want the skull shape to go and place the cardboard or stencil flat down on the jeans. Tape it down at the edges so it doesn't move around. Make some more tape rings and put them on the back of the pieces for the eyes and nose and attach them to the center of the stencil. Put on the rubber gloves, then use the bleach pen to color the inside of the stencil completely with a thick layer of bleach, making sure to go neatly around the eyes and nose. Press the stencil down tightly so bleach doesn't bleed under it.

5. Let it sit about 10 minutes. Then gently pull off the eyes and nose and slowly lift the stencil off the jeans, leaving behind a bleach-stained skull. Repeat the process if you want to add more than one skull to the jeans.

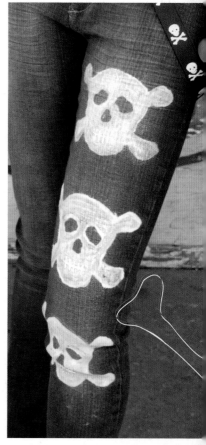

6. Let the jeans dry flat for at least 72 hours. Then wash your jeans alone in the washing machine to get the bleach smell out. (Make sure to wash them alone for the next two or three washes so you don't bleach any other clothes.)

7. When the jeans are clean and dry, lay them flat again and add a mouth with the fabric paint. Let dry at least 3 hours.

8. Clip on a pair of matching punky suspenders and hit the streets.

In-the-Army

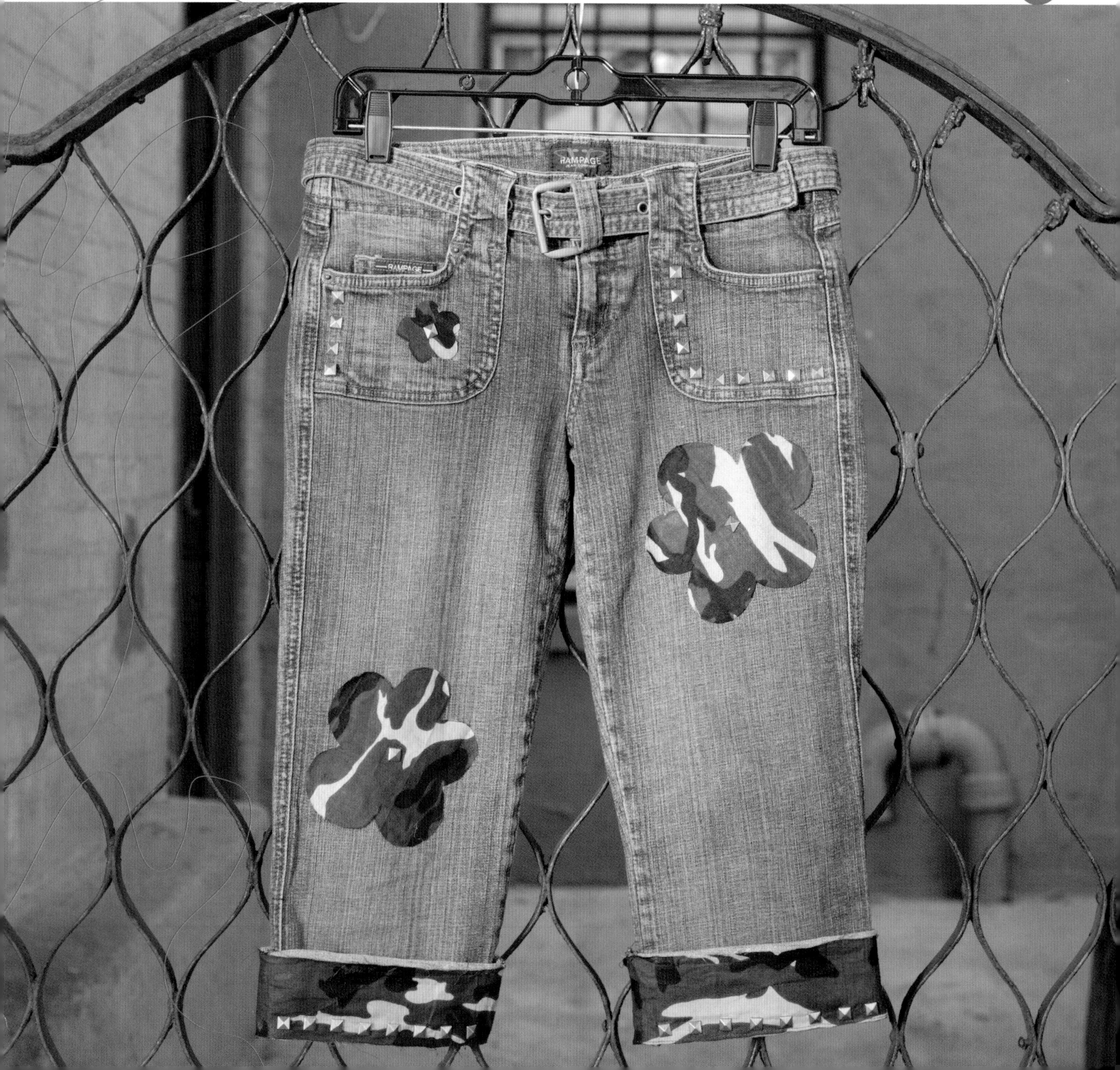

Camo Capris

Is your wardrobe feeling fatigued? These military-inspired capris will give it a quick pick-me-up! Camo print and tough gold studs make the perfect pair. Add some gold metallic accessories or an army-green cap, and you can guarantee that you won't blend into the crowd.

TAKE THIS

* pair of jeans
* seamstress chalk or fabric pencil
* ruler
* scissors
* iron and ironing board
* 1½ yards of cotton camo print fabric
* iron-on fusing tape (found at craft or sewing stores)
* scrap paper and pencil
* 1 package of gold pyramid studs
* washable fabric glue
* flathead screwdriver

MAKE THIS

1. Try the jeans on and decide how short you want them. Make a mark. Take the jeans off and lay them flat. Measure 5 inches below the mark you made and draw a straight, even line across. Cut along your line to shorten the leg. Repeat on the other leg.

2. Fold up the bottom of each leg twice to form a cuff, and iron in the crease.

3. Measure the height of one cuff, and its length going all the way around. Cut a piece of camo fabric the same measurements. Place the iron-on fusing tape on the back of the fabric. Line up the fabric neatly with the cuff and iron it down in place. Repeat for the other cuff.

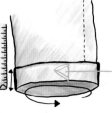

measure the width and the circumference of the cuff

4. Sketch out four or five bubble flower shapes in different sizes on scrap paper, or trace the template on page 140. When you like the way they look, cut them out and then trace around them onto the camo fabric. Cut the flowers out of the camo fabric.

5. Arrange the flowers on the front and back of the jeans however you like. Spread a thin layer of fabric glue over the back of each one and glue them down. Let the glue dry for 2 hours.

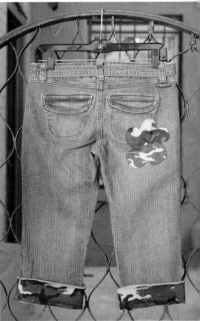

6. Take a gold stud and carefully press it through the center of one of the camo flowers, poking through both the flower and the denim. The stud has several sharp prongs in back that should go right through the fabric. Turn the jeans inside out so you can reach the inside of the leg, and use the flat edge of a standard screwdriver to press each prong down flat against the denim so it fastens in place. Repeat with the other flowers.

7. Use the same process to fasten gold studs along the front pockets and along the bottom edge of the cuffs. Put them on and salute your handiwork!

Knitty-

Gritty Jacket

If your old sweater and your denim jacket fell in love and had a kid, it would look something like this. You'll want to snuggle up with this super-cozy creation and never take it off. Layer it over a long-sleeve thermal and your favorite concert tee, or throw it over a girlie dress and some chunky boots for a tough-but-tender grunge rock look.

(tough) — washing symbols — (remove safety pins before washing)

TAKE THIS

* denim jacket
* old sweater or knit legwarmers for the sleeves
* old sweatshirt for the hood (optional)
* extra-large safety pins
* scissors
* straight pins
* sewing machine

MAKE THIS

1. Neatly cut the sleeves off the denim jacket, following the seams around the armholes to create a vest.

2. Neatly cut the arms off the sweater, following the seam around the armholes. (Or just keep the legwarmers as they are.)

3. Turn the vest inside out. Turn the sleeves or legwarmers inside out. Take the top of one of the sleeves and with your straight pins tack it down 1 inch in from the edge of the armhole. Stretch it a little to fit into the shape of the hole, pinning down the edge of the sweater as you go around. Make sure not to pin the hole closed accidentally.

4. When you are done, carefully machine-stitch the sweater in place. Go slowly, gathering the sweater if you need to in order to make it fit, and again making sure not to stitch the armhole shut!

5. Remove the straight pins and snip off any excess threads. Repeat on the other side with the other sleeve. Then turn the vest and both sleeves right-side out.

6. If you want to add a hood, cut it off the sweatshirt. Cut along the seam where it connects to the top part of the sweatshirt. Line one front edge of the hood up with the front edge of the jacket's collar and start pinning the hood on with the safety pins. You'll probably need about five or six pins to keep the hood on. (And whenever you don't want a hood, you can just unpin it to take it off!)

7. Pin a few large safety pins randomly around the front of the jacket as decoration.

JEANS RECYCLER

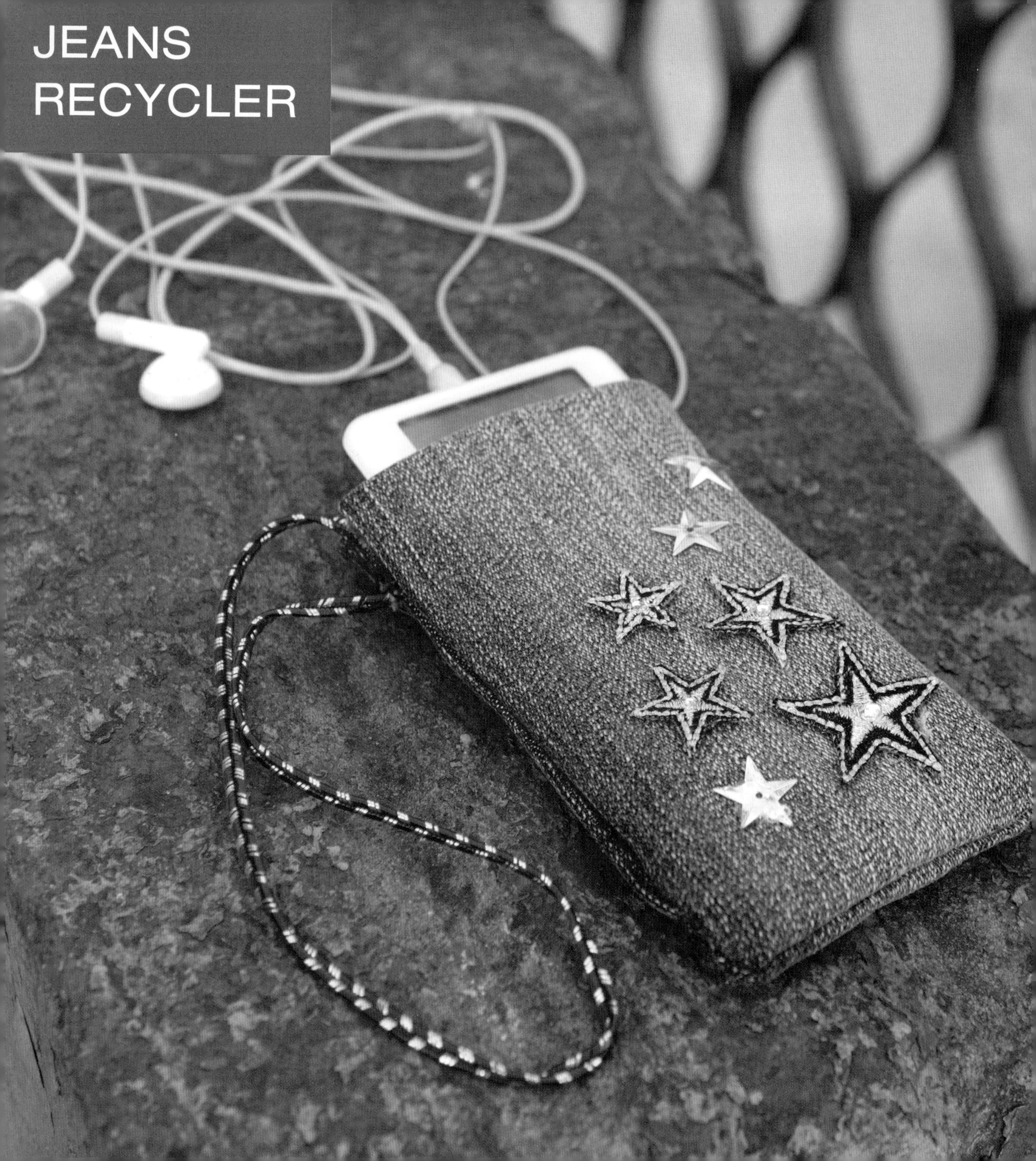

MP3-Cheers-for-Music Carrying Case

You probably take your music everywhere you go, so doesn't it deserve to look as cool as you do? Dress up your MP3 with this denim case and it will get as much attention as Angelina does from the paparazzi!

TAKE THIS

* **MP3 player**
* **pair of scrap jeans**
* **seamstress chalk or fabric pencil**
* **scissors**
* **½ yard of thin ribbon, cord, or chain**
* **measuring tape or ruler**
* **needle and thread (optional)**
* **sewing machine**
* **fabric glue**
* **assorted rhinestones, sequins, or appliqués**
* **fabric paint (optional)**

MAKE THIS

1. Place your MP3 player down flat on the jeans. Trace around the shape with the seamstress chalk. Using a ruler and the chalk, measure an extra ½ inch on all four sides and extend the pattern out.

2. Cut out the rectangle. Lay it on a new part of the jeans and trace around it. Cut a second identical rectangle out.

3. Hem one short end of each rectangle to get rid of the raw edge. Fold down the end ½ inch and machine- or hand-stitch it down. Repeat on the other piece of denim.

hem the top ends

4. Place the two pieces together, right sides facing in and hemmed ends at the top, and pin them in place. Machine-stitch a ¼-inch hem around the bottom and the two sides, leaving the top open so you can slide your MP3 player inside.

hem the two sides and the bottom

5. Cut off any loose threads. Gently turn the case right-side out. Use the tip of a scissors or pencil to help push down the bottom corners into place.

6. Cut a piece of ribbon or cord 14 inches long. Get your case and use scissors to make a tiny slit in one side seam, 1 inch below the top. Poke one end of the cord through the hole (if it won't fit, go back and snip a little more). Pull the cord through and knot the two ends together to create a loopy strap. Snip off any excess on the ends. Then slide the strap so the knot is hidden inside the case.

pull cord through slit and knot ends together

7. Decorate the front of the case by gluing on rhinestones and appliqués, or using fabric paint.

edgy 121

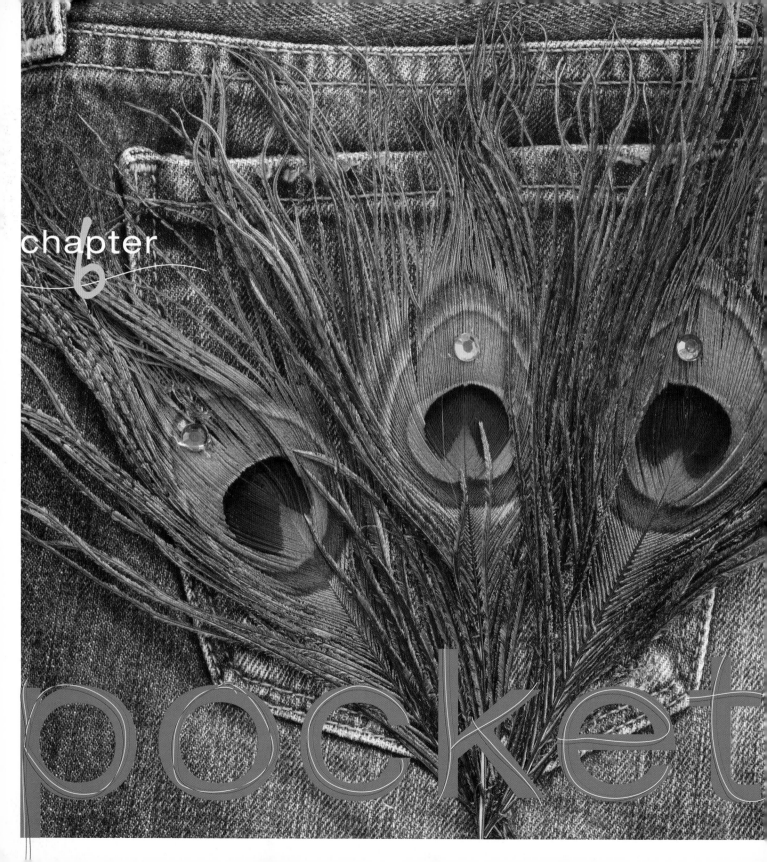

chapter

6

pocket

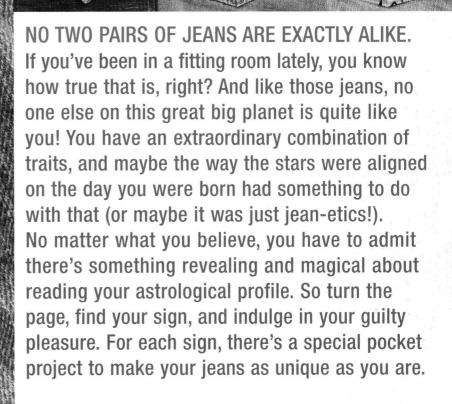

NO TWO PAIRS OF JEANS ARE EXACTLY ALIKE. If you've been in a fitting room lately, you know how true that is, right? And like those jeans, no one else on this great big planet is quite like you! You have an extraordinary combination of traits, and maybe the way the stars were aligned on the day you were born had something to do with that (or maybe it was just jean-etics!). No matter what you believe, you have to admit there's something revealing and magical about reading your astrological profile. So turn the page, find your sign, and indulge in your guilty pleasure. For each sign, there's a special pocket project to make your jeans as unique as you are.

astrologer

Aries

MARCH 21 TO APRIL 19

Symbol: The Ram

Power color: Red

Ruling planet: Mars

Element: Fire

FOR A DATE WORTH PUTTING YOUR JEANS ON, ASK OUT A: Leo or Sagittarius

FOR A DATE THAT WILL JUST GIVE YOU THE BLUES, AVOID A: Cancer or Virgo

CELEBRITY SOUL SISTERS: Danica Patrick, Reese Witherspoon, Sarah Jessica Parker

ARIES STAR STYLE TIP: Top off your denim with a fashion-forward fedora, a wide-brimmed newsboy cap, or any other cute hat.

YOUR PERSONALITY PROFILE: If Aries girls had a catch phrase it would be, "Me first!" You are all about taking charge, leading the way, and being first in line to try anything new. Your adventurous and courageous side pushes you to take risks, and your dynamic, charismatic personality inspires the people around you. This combination makes you a natural leader. You've got flames in your belly (and why wouldn't you—you're a fire sign!) and they fuel your need to compete and succeed. You love a challenge, whether it's physical (like a championship soccer match), intellectual (like acing an exam), or emotional (like getting a date with the most eligible guy on campus). In fact, the bigger the challenge, the more passionate you get. You play to win, staying fearless, enthusiastic, and strong right to the end.

YOUR POCKET PROJECT: It's all about you, so personalize your pants with your monogram! Go with red-and-white varsity-style letters to inspire your competitive spirit. Find iron-on letters at the craft store and pick out your initials. Read the directions on the package and iron each one on diagonally across the pocket. Then cut out two thin strips from a piece of felt and use fabric glue to attach them above and below the monogram.

Taurus

APRIL 20 TO MAY 20

Symbol: The Bull

Power color: Emerald green

Ruling planet: Venus

Element: Earth

FOR A DATE WORTH PUTTING YOUR JEANS ON, ASK OUT A: Virgo or Capricorn

FOR A DATE THAT WILL JUST GIVE YOU THE BLUES, AVOID A: Leo or Aquarius

CELEBRITY SOUL SISTERS: Audrey Hepburn, Uma Thurman, Renée Zellweger

TAURUS STAR STYLE TIP: Accessorize your denim with an intricate beaded necklace or a cool choker that highlights your throat.

YOUR PERSONALITY PROFILE: Taurus girls are tough cookies, and that's no bull! You are strong, determined, and passionate when it comes to getting a job done. You refuse to back down, no matter how big a challenge you're facing, and your independent, logical side keeps you centered and focused on the task at hand. Like your star sign, you can be stubborn and prefer to do things your way or no way, but your friends always look past that because you're also incredibly kind, generous, and fiercely loyal to those closest to you. While you work hard, you also know how to reward yourself. You have impeccable taste, appreciate nature and beauty, and love indulging your five senses in life's luxuries, like chocolate (yum!), mani-pedis (double yum!), and of course, designer jeans!

YOUR POCKET PROJECT: Spoil yourself silly with luxurious (faux!) fur pockets that you won't be able to stop petting. Neatly cut out a piece of fur the size and shape of your pocket. Spread a thin layer of fabric glue around the edges and fix it in place. Let it dry and repeat on the other side.

Gemini

MAY 21 TO JUNE 20

Symbol: The Twins

Power color: Yellow

Ruling planet: Mercury

Element: Air

FOR A DATE WORTH PUTTING YOUR JEANS ON, ASK OUT AN: Aquarius or Libra

FOR A DATE THAT WILL JUST GIVE YOU THE BLUES, AVOID A: Virgo or Pisces

CELEBRITY SOUL SISTERS: Natalie Portman, Mary-Kate and Ashley Olsen, Nicole Kidman

GEMINI STAR STYLE TIP: Pile on a handful of unusual rings and a wristful of interesting bracelets to complement all the wild hand gestures you make while talking!

YOUR PERSONALITY PROFILE: Gemini girls would make great spokespeople for cell phone companies—can you hear them now? You have the gift of gab and words come easily to you, whether you're debating with your friends, writing in your journal, or just babbling to yourself. Since you love to talk, you love having people to talk to. You connect quickly with others, and your Sidekick is overflowing with names, numbers, and e-mails for the friends you make everywhere you go. With your boundless energy and thirst for knowledge, you have your hands in a million different things all at once—but you get bored quickly. You are constantly changing and, like your star sign, it's almost as if there were two of you! Geminis hate to be tied down and need space for their restless spirits to fly freely in search of the next exciting person, place, or thing that will capture their attention.

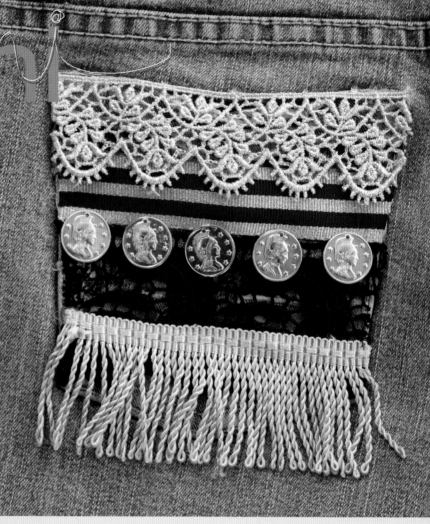

YOUR POCKET PROJECT: Create an eclectic patchwork of fabric, ribbons, and charms that's as unpredictable as you are. Since you're always changing, it will go with whatever your style happens to be that day. Cut several pieces of ribbon, lace, trim, or fabric and use fabric glue to attach them neatly across the pocket. Add buttons, charms, and extra details on top with fabric glue or a needle and thread. Let it dry and repeat on the other pocket with similar trims or something totally different and unexpected.

Cancer

JUNE 21 TO JULY 22

Symbol: The Crab

Power color: Metallic silver

Ruling planet: The Moon

Element: Water

FOR A DATE WORTH PUTTING YOUR JEANS ON, ASK OUT A: Scorpio or Pisces

FOR A DATE THAT WILL JUST GIVE YOU THE BLUES, AVOID A: Libra or Aries

CELEBRITY SOUL SISTERS: Liv Tyler, Pam Anderson, Jessica Simpson

CANCER STAR STYLE TIP: Pair your jeans with a midriff-baring sweater and a cropped jacket, then layer on some silver jewelry.

YOUR PERSONALITY PROFILE: Cancer chicks lead with their hearts, and their hearts always lead them back home. You're sensitive, emotional, and empathetic. You have a freaky ability to read people and sense exactly what they need, even before they do. These intuitive feelings sometimes get so strong that you've wondered if you might even be a bit psychic! (Come on, you know you have!) It wouldn't be a normal day if one of your friends weren't confiding in you or coming to you for advice or a comforting hug. You thrive on helping others, whether it's caring for a sibling, a pet, or even that little plant on your nightstand. And when you're not tending to friends or family, you're decorating and redecorating your bedroom, turning it into the perfect sanctuary. After worrying about everyone else, you cherish your privacy and need a place to hide away or deal with your moodiness. Because sometimes you can get a little, well, crabby! But deep down, everyone knows you're just a big softy.

YOUR POCKET PROJECT: You wear your heart on your sleeve, so why not wear it on your tush, too? Carefully remove the back pockets of your jeans. Use a seam ripper or the point of a scissors to remove the stitches so they fall away easily (make sure not to cut through the seat of the jeans). Cut a heart shape out of each pocket and then reattach them in place with a layer of fabric glue along the side and bottom edges but not the top—you don't want to glue the pockets shut. Add small round gold studs to look like pocket rivets.

Leo

JULY 23 TO AUGUST 22

Symbol: The Lion

Power color: Gold

Ruling planet: The Sun

Element: Fire

FOR A DATE WORTH PUTTING YOUR JEANS ON, ASK OUT AN: Aries or Sagittarius

FOR A DATE THAT WILL JUST GIVE YOU THE BLUES, AVOID A: Scorpio or Taurus

CELEBRITY SOUL SISTERS: Jennifer Lopez, Madonna, Halle Barry

LEO STAR STYLE TIP: Keep your jeans (and your fabulosity!) incognito—slip on a pair of dark, oversized movie star shades.

YOUR PERSONALITY PROFILE: If lions are the kings of the jungle, then Leo girls are the queens of the zodiac! Like your furry-maned astro mate, you're royal, confident, proud, and command respect everywhere you go. People are drawn to your magnetic personality and you make a fabulous, unforgettable first impression. Heads always swivel your way, whether you're performing on stage or just walking down the street. Good thing you love being the center of attention! Expressing yourself is priority number one, and your creativity comes out through song, dance, acting, writing, even your choice of clothes or the way you decorate your locker. You avoid anything that's status quo (boring!) and seek out the extraordinary, and when you find it you put one thousand percent into whatever you're doing. You live life to the fullest and love making a big splash, a dramatic entrance, or a unique statement. If it will get you applause or praise, you'll do it, but you don't let your ego get too big. Thankfully, you're also warmhearted, loyal, and caring, so your adoring fans will usually forgive you if you do!

YOUR POCKET PROJECT: Add a little bling to your backside and you'll attract even more attention! Use fabric glue to decorate the edges of the pocket with rhinestones. Find a premade iron-on or sticky-backed rhinestone decal at a craft store—one with a crown is perfect for you, princess! Iron it onto the center of the pocket or, if it has a sticky back, add a layer of fabric glue to strengthen the hold. Repeat on the other pocket and let it dry.

Virgo

AUGUST 23 TO SEPTEMBER 22

Symbol: The Virgin

Power color: Navy blue

Ruling planet: Mercury

Element: Earth

FOR A DATE WORTH PUTTING YOUR JEANS ON, ASK OUT A: Taurus or Capricorn

FOR A DATE THAT WILL JUST GIVE YOU THE BLUES, AVOID A: Gemini or Sagittarius

CELEBRITY SOUL SISTERS: Michelle Williams, Cameron Diaz, Beyoncé Knowles

VIRGO STAR STYLE TIP: Turn your jeans into smarty-pants and wear them with a pair of funky wire-rimmed or tortoise shell glasses. (If you don't normally wear them, get a fake pair at the dollar store or drugstore!)

YOUR PERSONALITY PROFILE: Virgo girls are as close to perfection as you can get. You're methodical, efficient, and neat, and you feel totally out of sorts when things are out of order. Your detail-oriented, super-organizer side shows in everything you do, from your color-coordinated closet to the alphabetized DVDs lined up on your bookshelf. Just try not to obsess too much! You love making lists, but probably love crossing things off them even more. As a conscientious, hard worker, there's nothing more satisfying to you than a job well done. You can be a bit of a health nut so you enjoy rewarding yourself with an organic meal, a new yoga class, or a facial with an all-natural beauty scrub. At first glance you seem reserved, but only those closest to you discover your complex, sensitive, and emotional side. You may be a woman of few words, but when you speak you appear intelligent, witty, and often profound—and those around better listen up!

YOUR POCKET PROJECT: The perfectionist in you will love lining up the ribbons in this grid until they are exactly spaced out and even. Pick two or three different-colored or patterned ribbons. Make sure they are thin or the grid will get too sloppy. Cut about ten strips—five go vertically and five go horizontally. Lay them out on the pocket to create the grid. If you need more, cut a few more pieces. When you are ready, use fabric glue to attach them neatly in place. Cut off any excess from the edges and let dry. Repeat on the other pocket.

Libra

SEPTEMBER 23 TO OCTOBER 22

Symbol: The Scales

Power color: Pink

Ruling planet: Venus

Element: Air

FOR A DATE WORTH PUTTING YOUR JEANS ON, ASK OUT AN: Aquarius or Gemini

FOR A DATE THAT WILL JUST GIVE YOU THE BLUES, AVOID A: Cancer or Capricorn

CELEBRITY SOUL SISTERS: Gwyneth Paltrow, Brigitte Bardot, Kate Winslet

LIBRA STAR STYLE TIP: Balance the casual vibe of your jeans by slipping them on over a pair of luxuriously silky undies and a matching bra.

YOUR PERSONALITY PROFILE: Libra girls never lose their balance. Like the scales that represent your sign, you carefully weigh all sides of every decision. You're a born problem solver, and when you're faced with a challenge, you can't sleep until you've figured out the best solution. Sometimes you think so long that you avoid making any decision, but you're levelheaded and smart, so follow your gut and you'll always make the right choice. You're happiest when all the pieces of your life fit together smoothly, like a puzzle, and everyone is getting along. When there's conflict, you do your very best to avoid it. Instead, you rely on your diplomacy, charm, and excellent communication skills to create harmony among those around you. Your amazing knack for bringing people together makes you a master party planner and a great matchmaker. When you send out an evite, your RSVP inbox overflows. Just make sure to save one of those party guests for yourself—you prefer being part of a romantic couple to flying solo, so pour on the charm and chat up that cutie standing by the nachos!

YOUR POCKET PROJECT: You are simply charming and now your pocket can be, too! Hit the jewelry aisle of a craft store and look for little charms like hearts, stars, jingle bells, or mini picture frames to display photos of your friends. Use a needle and thread to stitch each charm along the top edge of the pocket. Make sure not to stitch through the seat of the jeans or you'll sew the pocket shut. Repeat on the other side.

Scorpio

OCTOBER 23 TO NOVEMBER 21

Symbol: The Scorpion

Power color: Black

Ruling planet: Mars

Element: Water

FOR A DATE WORTH PUTTING YOUR JEANS ON, ASK OUT A: Virgo or Capricorn

FOR A DATE THAT WILL JUST GIVE YOU THE BLUES, AVOID A: Leo or Aquarius

CELEBRITY SOUL SISTERS: Chloe Sevigny, Parker Posey, Julia Roberts

SCORPIO STAR STYLE TIP: Toughen up your denim with a beat-up black leather jacket and a cool (temporary!) tat.

YOUR PERSONALITY PROFILE: Scorpio babes are like riddles wrapped in enigmas! You are incredibly complex and secretive, and it takes a long time to get to know the real you. There's a powerful intensity that surrounds you, and you experience everyday life at a deeper level than any other sign. You are passionate and fiery and give off a naturally sexy vibe even if you're not trying to, a sort of alluring mystery that intrigues others. People want to be around your aura and rightly so—you make a wonderful listener and a fiercely loyal friend. But if someone crosses you, look out! With the stubborn grudges you hold, it'll be hard for you to ever forgive them. Although you keep your true feelings hidden, you have a highly active inner world and your emotions run deep. In fact, they almost control you. Use your willpower and ambition to help keep them in check so you can stay focused. You are intuitive, clever, and persistent, and you love the challenge of a good mystery, like figuring out who's guilty on an episode of CSI before it ends, or uncovering that secret you know your best friend has been keeping from you.

YOUR POCKET PROJECT: Spider webs are dark and complex, and although they seem a little spooky, they're also intriguing—just like you! Pick a web print fabric (you'll find the best selection around Halloween time). Cut a square out and trim it to fit neatly over the pocket. Place a thin layer of glue around just the edges and glue it in place. Glue one lone rhinestone in the center of one of the webs to add extra allure. Repeat with the other pocket.

Sagittarius

NOVEMBER 22 TO DECEMBER 21

Symbol: The Archer

Power color: Purple

Ruling planet: Jupiter

Element: Fire

FOR A DATE WORTH PUTTING YOUR JEANS ON, ASK OUT A: Aries or Leo

FOR A DATE THAT WILL ONLY GIVE YOU THE BLUES, AVOID A: Pisces or Virgo

CELEBRITY SOUL SISTERS: Katie Holmes, Christina Aguilera, Tyra Banks

SAGITTARIUS STAR STYLE TIP: Stylish sneakers and a trendy tote or backpack make the perfect traveling companions for your jeans.

YOUR PERSONALITY PROFILE: Like the arrow your star sign shoots, Sagittarius girls need to fly free. You're an independent spirit with a burning desire to travel and explore unknown places and ideas. Nothing scares you more than being tied down or stuck in a rut, and you get restless quickly. Since you're always on the move it can be hard to keep a lot of friends. But when you do spend time with people—even if only for a few moments— they are deeply affected by your charisma and kindness. You're open-minded and curious and are fascinated by anything foreign, exotic, artistic, or unusual. Whether you are having an adventure out in the real world or are just reading a profound book, you love to learn and are always on a quest for truth, knowledge, and spiritual enlightenment. If you're ever faced with a problem, you trust in the universe and feel that it will help you make decisions if you listen to the signs it's giving you. When you need to unwind, want some space, or crave time alone with your philosophical thoughts, you head for the great outdoors to do something athletic, like hiking or biking.

YOUR POCKET PROJECT: Make your jeans look like you brought them back from a foreign bazaar in a far-off land with a trio of exotic peacock feathers. Buy a package in a craft store and attach each one with a few small blobs of fabric glue on the back. (Don't use too much glue or the feathers will get gooey and ruined.) Let them dry completely. Decorate the feathers with a few colorful rhinestones or sequins. Repeat on the other side or just decorate one pocket, since these are pretty bold!

Capricorn

DECEMBER 22 TO JANUARY 19

Symbol: The Goat

Power color: Chocolate brown

Ruling planet: Saturn

Element: Earth

FOR A DATE WORTH PUTTING YOUR JEANS ON, ASK OUT A: Virgo or Taurus

FOR A DATE THAT WILL ONLY GIVE YOU THE BLUES, AVOID AN: Aries or Libra

CELEBRITY SOUL SISTERS: Kate Moss, Christy Turlington, Katie Couric

CAPRICORN STAR STYLE TIP: Pair your jeans with a classic cashmere sweater to look polished and timeless. Don't forget to pop that lip balm you can't live without into your pocket!

YOUR PERSONALITY PROFILE: Get out of the way! Capricorn gals are on the express track to Successville. You're a super-achiever and, like the mountain goat that represents your sign, you look a rocky uphill climb right in the face and slowly but surely claw your way to the glorious view at the top. No goal you set for yourself is too ambitious, and with your self-discipline, organizational skills, patience, and drive you'll work as hard as it takes to reach it. When things don't go your way you can get a little bossy and pessimistic, but overall you adapt well to setbacks, learning from them and becoming even stronger than before. You love taking on responsibility, but you're also motivated by the recognition, prestige, and fame that come from accomplishing something big. You're destined for a career in the spotlight—think CEO, politician, or movie star. Even though you're usually serious, down-to-earth, and practical, you also know how to let your hair down after a long day, when your dry sense of humor comes out to play.

YOUR POCKET PROJECT: You set your sights high and are always reaching for the moon and stars. Motivate yourself with your own little celestial scene. Cut a moon shape out of shiny fabric and use fabric glue to attach it to your back pocket. Glue a bunch of star-shaped sequins around the moon. Then go back and neatly outline the moon with silvery fabric paint and add a dot of gold fabric paint in the center of each star. Let dry completely. Repeat on the other pocket if you like.

Aquarius

JANUARY 20 TO FEBRUARY 18

Symbol: The Water Bearer

Power color: Electric blue

Ruling planet: Uranus

Element: Air

FOR A DATE WORTH PUTTING YOUR JEANS ON, ASK OUT A: Libra or Gemini

FOR A DATE THAT WILL ONLY GIVE YOU THE BLUES, AVOID A: Scorpio or Taurus

CELEBRITY SOUL SISTERS: Jennifer Aniston, Oprah Winfrey, Christina Ricci

AQUARIUS STAR STYLE TIP: Show off a pair of cute patterned socks or tights and ankle boots from underneath cropped or cuffed jeans.

YOUR PERSONALITY PROFILE: Aquarian girls are truly one of a kind. You're original, creative, and maybe even a little eccentric. But you're too busy marching to your own drummer to worry what others think. You're constantly dreaming up revolutionary ideas, wacky schemes, and out-of-the-box plans, and thinking of ways to implement them. With your insightful vision and kind, altruistic nature, you're determined to change the world. A sense of community is important to you, as well as building strong friendships, so you're involved up to your eyeballs in clubs, volunteer opportunities, and group projects, where you hope to meet diverse people and make a difference. When you find a cause close to your heart, you grab on and won't let go. Although you're open-minded and optimistic, you're also highly opinionated, and if someone disagrees with you, you can get a little snotty. Like the hippie Age of Aquarius, you can also be spiritual, earthy, and even a bit psychic. When you need a mental break from saving the planet, you surprise friends with your offbeat humor and your rebellious, unpredictable outbursts.

YOUR POCKET PROJECT: Nothing captures your earthy, hippie spirit better than beautiful butterflies. Find several iron-on patches at a craft store. Read the directions on the back and iron them on to the pocket. Place one off-center, as if it's flying off the pocket and "out of the box," just like you! Repeat on the other pocket if desired.

Pisces

FEBRUARY 19 TO MARCH 20

Symbol: The Fish

Power color: Sea green

Ruling planet: Neptune

Element: Water

FOR A DATE WORTH PUTTING YOUR JEANS ON, ASK OUT A: Cancer or Scorpio

FOR A DATE THAT WILL ONLY GIVE YOU THE BLUES, AVOID A: Gemini or Sagittarius

CELEBRITY SOUL SISTERS: Drew Barrymore, Mia Hamm, Queen Latifah

PISCES STAR STYLE TIP: Let your beautiful feet complement your denim. Pair jean skirts with strappy sandals, flip-flops, or peep-toe pumps and a perfect pedicure.

YOUR PERSONALITY PROFILE: Pisces girls float through life in a dreamy, introspective bubble. You're compassionate, gentle, shy, and emotional. Your intuitive soul is so hypersensitive that you pick up on and absorb whatever mood is going on around you. If someone you know is feeling sad, all of a sudden you'll be unhappy, too. Your friends appreciate how empathetic you are. People automatically relax around you and enjoy your calming presence, so you're probably pretty popular. But sometimes you get so emotional it can be hard to deal with; you need time alone to escape into the fantasy worlds of your favorite movies, books, magazines, or songs. You devour anything creative since it all helps fuel your own fantastic and vivid daydreams. Just be aware when you're drifting off—you tend to lose track of time and the things going on around you when your mind wanders, so you might get a rep as a space cadet. Like the water your finned astro mate swims in, you are always changing and need to avoid anything routine, but you'll stay connected to your inner dream world forever.

YOUR POCKET PROJECT: Your fantastic daydreams can take you around the world or over the rainbow. Add this colorful icon to your pocket, and don't forget the fluffy clouds to drift away on! Cut arch shapes out of colored felt. Use fabric glue to attach them in rainbow-color order onto the pocket. Then cut out two felt clouds and add them as well. Repeat on the other side, let dry, and dream on.

templates

The following pages have five templates for the projects in the book that require them.

Trace this template to make the heart on the back of the **Wild-at-Heart Jacket** on page 84.

Here's a slithering snake
template to use for making the
Serpentine Skirt on page 102.

Use these star templates to
make the **Superstar Jeans**
on page 106.

This skull and bones template is for making
the Punky Pirate Jeans on page 114.

These flower templates are for making
the **In-the-Army Camo Capris**
on page 116.

resources

FOR CRAFT SUPPLIES:

A.C. MOORE
Stores nationwide
www.acmoore.com

DOLLAR FABRIC.COM
Inexpensive fabric by the yard.

350 Manhattan Ave.
Brooklyn, NY 11211
800-991-9897
www.dollarfabric.com

HOME DEPOT
Stores nationwide
www.homedepot.com

JO-ANN FABRIC AND CRAFT STORES
Stores nationwide
www.joann.com

MICHAELS
Stores nationwide
www.michaels.com

M&J TRIMMING
Amazing trims, lace, ribbon, appliqués, and more.

1008 6th Avenue
New York, NY 10018
800-9MJTRIM
www.mjtrim.com

PLAID ENTERPRISES INC.
This company manufactures loads of paints, stencils, glues, and other craft supplies, including a line of cool iron-ons just for denim.

800-842-4197
www.plaidonline.com

REPRODEPOT FABRICS
Very cute fabrics, pins, ribbons, and appliqués.

877-RETROFAB
www.reprodepotfabrics.com

2 BEAD OR NOT 2 BEAD
Big selection of basic and unusual beads.

1234 Western Avenue
Albany, NY 12203
(866) 733-5233
www.2beadornot2bead.com

FOR INEXPENSIVE JEANS:

Thrift stores: Find a local branch of one of these giant charitable organizations online, and then scope them out often to get great, cheap finds.

GOODWILL INDUSTRIES INTERNATIONAL
www.goodwill.org

SALVATION ARMY
www.salvationarmyusa.org

Retail stores:
KOHL'S
www.kohls.com

RAINBOW SHOPS
www.rainbowshops.com

WET SEAL
www.wetseal.com

KMART
www.kmart.com

JC PENNEY
www.jcpenney.com

JOYCE LESLIE
Stores in the northeast
www.joyceleslie.com

FOR STORAGE:

THE CONTAINER STORE
This is an organizer's dream store. They have boxes, bins, carts, containers, and every size and color storage solution imaginable to keep your craft supplies orderly.

Stores nationwide
www.containerstore.com

TARGET
They have cute and inexpensive bins, baskets, and other storage ideas and of course cute jeans, too!

Stores nationwide
800-800-8800
www.target.com

acknowledgments

This book could never have come together without the help of many wonderful and dedicated people. To start, I would like to send a million and one thank-yous to Julie Mazur for taking a chance on a first-time author, for her unending patience, and for believing in my vision and allowing me so much creative freedom. Thank you to Cathy Hennessy for her excellent editor's eye and to Kathleen Jacques for her precise and helpful illustrations. Thank you to Julie Duquet and Margo Mooney for their inJEANious artistic prowess and for the beautiful design of this book. And a huge debt of gratitude to the rest of the Watson-Guptill staff for their enthusiasm and support and for all their tireless work in getting this book off the ground.

I would also like to send a big hug and lots of love to Jessica Blatt for recommending me for this project and without whom none of this would have happened.

A huge thank-you goes to the following companies for their generous denim donations: Silver Jeans, US Polo Association, Plugg, Iron Jeans, and Rampage.

An enormous thank-you to the following super-cool people who helped bring my projects to life on the pages of this book, for being so patient during the very long photo shoot, and for making the day so much fun: Sonya Farrell, photographer extraordinaire; her trusty photo assistants, Whitney Dunnigan and Carrie Comfort; makeup and hair stylist Maki Hasegawa; Amanda Perez, my assistant fashion stylist; and the beautiful and energetic models, Alissa, Darcy, Darren, Derrick, Kristy, and Natasha.

A great big shout-out and thanks to the entire staff (past and present) of CosmoGIRL! magazine for turning me into a DIY guru, for inspiring me creatively every day for six and a half years, for teaching me to think big, and for pushing me to be the best I could possibly be.

A special heartfelt thanks goes to every single one of my friends and family for their endless encouragement, love, and emotional support, and especially to Dana and Jay E., Joanna K., Kristen S., Lauren B., Raina K., Rick B., and Ted P., for their brilliant creative help, their clothing donations, their editorial expertise, and for just being there for me whenever I needed them throughout this entire process.

And last but definitely not least, an incredibly special thank-you and all my love to my wonderful parents, Ilene and Marvin Greene, for encouraging me to grow personally and professionally, for always supporting my decisions, for putting up with me when I get stressed out and a little crazy, and of course for indulging my love of fashion and buying me my first pair of designer jeans at age four!

Photograph by Allan Reider

index